ORGANIZED
CLOSETS &
STORAGE

IDEAS FOR EVERY ROOM IN YOUR HOUSE

STEPHANIE CULP

Writer's Digest Books

Cincinnati, Ohio

Organized Closets & Storage: Ideas for Every Room in Your House.
Copyright © 1990 by Stephanie Culp. Printed and bound in the United
States of America. All rights reserved. No part of this book may be repro-
duced in any form or by any electronic or mechanical means including
information storage and retrieval systems without permission in writing
from the publisher, except by a reviewer, who may quote brief passages
in a review. Published by Writer's Digest Books, an imprint of F&W
Publications, Inc., 1507 Dana Ave., Cincinnati, Ohio 45207. First edition.

94 93 92 91 90   5 4 3 2 1

Library of Congress Cataloging-in-Publication Data

Culp, Stephanie.
   Organized closets & storage : ideas for every room in your house/
Stephanie Culp.
      p.   cm.
   ISBN 0-89879-390-4
   1. Storage in the home. 2. Clothes closets. I. Title. II. Title: Orga-
nized closets and storage.
TX309.C85   1989   89-38840
648'.8 — dc20   CIP

Design by Carol Buchanan

To James (Jim) Ronald Reed with Love

Contents

Acknowledgments

Now that I've written several books, I've noticed that some of the same terrific people are there for me each time. At Writer's Digest Books, Jo Hoff provides an enthusiastic link, and Mert Ransdell makes the business of being a writer remarkably simple and pleasant. Beth Franks, freelance editor extraordinaire, provides that all important guiding hand, giving the book the organization and direction that it would not otherwise have. Special love and gratitude are due the two constants in my life for providing company, amusement, support, and love during the writing process — Jim Reed and Fritz.

Some special newcomers have contributed to the effort: JBL Graphics in Montrose, California, managed the information that went into the Resource Guide, and Barbara Adelman organized the many photographs that were submitted. Special thanks goes to the space planners, designers, retailers, and manufacturers of closet and storage products who provided the many photographs that have added so much to the book. I'm also most appreciative of the experts who so willingly shared their expertise with me for inclusion in this book. Special thanks also to John Andraud for his good-humored and patient assistance in the production process.

Introduction

Closet and other storage space in the home is always in demand. There never seems to be enough of this vital space, and yet, as a professional organizer, I know that if you take a fresh look at the situation, there is usually more potential space than you realize. This book will take you on a walking tour of every room in your house, to help you assess your current closet and storage capacity. We'll address all the storage problems encountered in the average home, and consider various solutions.

For example, maximizing your closet and storage space may mean sifting through your belongings and weeding out what is no longer appropriate to your lifestyle. It may also mean rethinking and reorganizing how and where you store things. Or it could mean installing some space-saving systems and cabinetry to increase the storage space you already have. You may even want to remodel and/or redecorate, to give yourself that much needed extra closet or storage space and give the room an updated look at the same time.

Organized Closets and Storage is jam-packed with practical ideas for expanding your available storage space, with dozens of photographs of space-saving systems and products that are available for you to use creatively in your design for storage success. In addition, I consulted eight experts on how to deal effectively with specific storage problems. These special "Tips from the Pros" will help you with everything from how to find the right storage products and systems to how to organize the things you are now storing.

Finally, after you've considered all the options and you're ready to roll up your sleeves and expand your available space, the last chapter provides an eight-step plan for storage success. Used in conjunction with the ideas found throughout the book, this plan will help you reach your goal to increase or maximize your closet and storage space. The Resource Guide follows the plan, to make shopping for products and services easier.

A realistic approach, teamed with some creative ideas and organization, can often yield exciting results. With this book as your planning guide to more closet and storage space, I wish you much success!

A hall closet can be turned into a "sports center" to provide effective storage for apartment dwellers who have no garage or basement to store their sporting equipment. Acknowledgment: Techline by Marshall Erdman & Associates, Madison, Wisconsin. Photo by Steven Rhyner.

Chapter 1:
Halls and Foyers

Extra space often lurks in the most unexpected places. You may actually have some unexploited space right inside your front door or in an upstairs hallway. Although halls and foyers are often overlooked as potential storage areas, there is generally a spare closet in the vicinity. With a little imagination you can convert some of that open space into an extension of the closet. For instance, the traditional coat and hat tree, placed in a foyer corner, can be the resting place for outdoor gear that's used on a daily basis (jackets, scarves, caps). Pegs or a mug rack on the back of the spare closet door can provide even more hanging space. An umbrella stand provides organized storage for dripping umbrellas; an attractive basket on a small table (or tucked in the drawer) will keep gloves together and ready to go.

Many halls will accommodate a narrow bookcase which could hold all of your paperbacks or cassette or videotapes. A shelf along the molding at the top of the wall might also hold paperback books, without interfering with the space in the hall itself. In a back hallway, a pegboard and hook or grid and hook system will accommodate hanging items such as sports equipment or school book bags. You can even hang a bike from hooks on the wall if you are a city apartment dweller. If your hall is really large, you might put an armoire or other newer, freestanding wardrobe in the area. Other possibilities include a pretty chest of drawers, trunk, cabinet, or wall unit system—where just about anything you want to store can be accommodated.

If you have a staircase off the foyer, check the space under the stairs; you may have enough room for a small dresser or trunk or some modular cubes or even a work table for hobbies and crafts. A storage bench with cushions can provide a reading nook for a child if you mount a small lamp on the wall by the bench. Customizing possibilities include building in a wine rack, installing hooks and bins for sports gear (this is a good spot for the bike), or building slots for oversized artwork or for storing suitcases. If you want to enclose the space so that the things stored are hidden, hire a qualified cabinetmaker to design and install doors. Conversely, if the area under the stairs is currently closed off, often this wall is easy to knock out and replace with doors, opening up that extra bit of storage space that had been hidden—and wasted.

Hall Closet

Originally meant to hold coats, hall closets can harbor all manner of things, in and out of season. Tennis rackets, slide carrousels, hiking boots, shopping bags, suitcases, holiday decorations, board games, and the vacuum cleaner all vie for space in many of America's overstuffed hall closets. Throw in a box of tax records along with some coats, hats, and boots, and suddenly getting the vacuum cleaner out presents the ultimate challenge, since invariably it starts a cascading effect that is more aggravating than the chore at hand.

To cut down on the congestion in the closet and still make use of it for efficient storage, the first step is to eliminate unnecessary clutter. Old papers, outgrown clothes, broken appliances and toys, and all of the other totally useless junk should be tossed or given away. That done, you'll want to design a closet system that will save the maximum amount of space. For instance, if your front closet is given over mostly to coats and jackets, you might benefit from a combination of double rod and single rod systems which will give you more room for all of your jackets and still accommodate a few long coats. Shelving should (in most cases) be expanded upon by adding another shelf or two at the top of the closet. Hooks on the side walls, at the back of the closet, and on the inside of the closet door can also hold anything hangable. Rolling basket systems (which come in various sizes and heights) can be used to hold everything from boots and mittens to sports gear.

A word of warning: Although the hall closet has tremendous potential for storage, if you're trying to fit shopping bags, old tax records, games, skis, coats, sports equipment, luggage, pet equipment, and anything else you can cram into it, you're asking for trouble. That closet is not in itself a storage miracle, so don't use it as a dumping ground for anything and everything. Give careful thought to what you *need* to organize and store there, and then look to other areas for solutions, such as the basement, garage, laundry, or children's rooms. Special storage centers in all of those areas can help lighten the hall closet load and keep everything nicely organized and accessible at the same time.

This over-the-door rack fits easily on either the inside or the outside of the hall closet door. Acknowledgment: Spectrum Diversified Design, Inc., Cleveland, Ohio.

Holiday Decorations and Gift Wrap

Holiday decorations and gift wrap often come to rest in the spare closet, and frequently get squashed beyond recognition and serviceability. Some decorations accumulate year by year until you find yourself with five times more than you'll ever use—all of it crammed into the hall closet. Face the holiday facts, and give yourself more storage space by getting rid of the stuff you never use. The things that are kept year round in this closet, particularly the gift wrap, should then be stored so that you can retrieve whatever you need whenever you need it.

Boxes. People tend to save gift boxes thinking they'll recycle them at a holiday. Inevitably only a few get reused and the rest get pushed and shoved around in the closet. Save a half dozen boxes if you must, but make sure that they all fit into one another to cut down on the shelf space required.

Paper. You can reduce the amount of gift wrap on hand if you buy all occasion paper. Glossy white paper with a pretty ribbon will do just as well at Christmas as it will for a wedding or a birthday; a red-striped paper will cover all of those and Valentine's Day as well. All occasion paper can be used throughout the year, so store it where it is readily accessible. You can segregate it in the closet (so it won't get squashed) by storing it in a gift wrap organizer, available from mail order catalogs. These handy organizers are made of heavy cardboard and assemble into an organizer with special compartments to hold rolls of paper, flat paper, and spools of ribbon. Another option is to stand rolls up in a small plastic trash can. Flat paper can be stored in a plastic sweater box and put on a shelf, or if you have drawer space (in a small chest of drawers in the hall, or in a rolling basket system in the closet) you can store the flat paper and ribbon there. Scissors and tape can be hung on a small cup hook in the closet or stored with ribbon in a plastic sweater or shoe box.

Miscellaneous Decorations. Store out-of-season decorations in boxes on the highest shelf in the closet, labeled clearly by holiday. You can also store these boxes under a bed, or, if you must, in the garage or attic, but only if these areas are very clean. Ornaments should be stored in ornament boxes (so they'll be intact next year when you need them), and lights can be looped around a piece of cardboard and stored in labeled boxes as well.

Sports Equipment

If your hall closet has turned into a sports center, you can increase the storage space and organize the gear by adding shelves, hooks, and rolling baskets or bins. Bins marked "swim gear," "camping gear," or "tennis balls" will keep things together so that getting what you need for any sports activity is simple, and putting the gear away when it needs to be stored—for however long—is equally simple. Hooks can hold things like rackets and mitts, and a plastic trash can makes a good depository for balls of all sizes.

Suitcases

If your suitcases are stored in this closet, stop to review how many you own. If you only use a special few, get rid of excess baggage so you have adequate space to store the bags you do need (or something else that you actually *use*). These can be stored on a top shelf, and garment bags can be hung on hooks at the back of the closet. If you are squeezed for space in this closet, remember that you can also store luggage under the stairs, under the bed, and on closet shelves in other rooms that are too high up for practical daily use. Or store some of your suitcases inside a trunk or foot locker (the foot locker may fit sideways into the closet, under the stairs, or in a corner of the hall). You can also store soft-sided luggage inside other luggage, so that three suitcases occupy the space of one.

Vacuum Cleaner Parts

Vacuum cleaner parts tend to get separated from the vacuum cleaner, which is usually stored in this closet for lack of any better storage options in the house. Then, when you need that special gizmo to clean some corner or crevice, you can't find the necessary piece in the closet. To more effectively store these items, use an attachment bag or rack that hangs in the closet or mounts on the closet wall or inside door. Or you can simply throw the parts in a bin (such as a dishpan or kitty litter pan) which is kept on the closet shelf or floor. (A shallow pan with parts can also be stored under a bed if space in the closet is limited.) And, get rid of exotic attachments you know you will never use. Vacuuming is a chore, not an art.

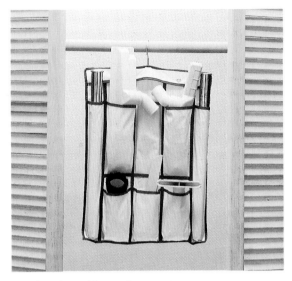

This handy caddy neatly organizes vacuum cleaner accessories and can be hung on the hall closet rod or on a hook or rack mounted on the inside of the hall closet door. Acknowledgment: Metropolitan Vacuum Cleaner Co., Suffern, New York.

These storage units are designed to be a focal point of the room. The overhead lighting accents the decorative aspects of the painting over the fireplace as well as the two surrounding cabinets. Acknowledgment: Wood-Mode Cabinetry.

Chapter 2:
Living Room

The living room may or may not actually be "lived in." The formal living room is used only for entertaining guests; homes with formal living rooms often have family rooms, and that's where the family congregates to watch television, play games, and spend time together. Homes without family rooms must use the living room for both everyday family activities and for entertaining, so the space must be more versatile and organized. Studio apartments really put the "living" room concept to the test. Since the studio has basically only one room (plus the bath and kitchen), everything needs to be accommodated in this area, from sleeping to everyday living to formal entertaining needs. For those living rooms that are used every day, storage facilities can be integrated into the overall decor to add function to the room and/or provide that additional space needed to hold items that won't fit into the storage facilities in other rooms in the house.

Before you consider your storage options, take a good hard look at the furniture in the room. Great Grandma's Victorian settee, two more lamps than are necessary, and itty-bitty antique tables may have nostalgia value, but they leave you shortchanged on function. Credenzas, buffets, trunks, bookshelves, and end tables with drawers and cabinet space can serve you much better — doing double duty as furniture and storage space simultaneously.

A buffet, for instance, doesn't have to be in the dining room — it can be placed along a wall in the living room and used to store videotapes, records, books, or games. Even a coffee table can be functional. A table with a shelf on the bottom can hold magazines, knickknacks, newspapers, and the *TV Guide*, doubling the space of the table and eliminating clutter on the top of the table by providing storage underneath. Or a piece of glass on top of a wicker or antique trunk turns into a coffee table or end table that can also be used to store any number of infrequently used things — from games to blankets or memorabilia. If you are going to use tables at the end of the sofa, end tables with drawers or shelves are just as attractive as those without the extra storage features.

In the studio apartment, convertible sofas and futons, Murphy Wallbeds, and single beds dressed with a tailored cover and bolster will save space or do double duty — as the sofa by day and bed by night. Captain's beds with built-in storage drawers provide the bed and space to hold the linens all in one unit.

Cabinetry and Shelving

Cabinetry and shelving can be incorporated into the living room in a number of ways. Floor-to-ceiling wall units that include cabinets at the bottom and open shelves at the top can hold lots of different things. Closed cabinetry at the bottom of the wall unit can gracefully store things like games, tapes, slides, and even knitting supplies behind closed doors,

This heavy-duty modular storage system can be assembled in less than ten minutes and can be a simple solution for storing books, entertainment equipment, and decorative items in the living room. Acknowledgment: Professional's Choice™ Shelving for the living room.

while shelves provide the open space needed to display sculptures, books, small antiques, mementos, photos, and knickknacks. If the sofa is floated in the room, it can be backed with a bookcase that stands as tall as the couch. Used rather than end tables, this can give you a surface immediately adjacent to the seating area for a lamp, magazines, or attractive decorative items. Since the back of the bookcase is against the sofa, the shelves can be used for books or other decorative items. Studio apartment dwellers can use a wall unit — from a freestanding two-shelf bookcase to a floor-to-ceiling unit — to separate the living area into functions, i.e., living and dining, living and sleeping, or living and study/office areas.

You can even design a custom do-it-yourself wall unit that incorporates a chest of drawers or a trunk. The trunk can hold out-of-season sweaters or blankets, while the chest of drawers holds underwear, stockings, or any other miscellaneous items that might not fit in the closet. You might profit from a table that folds down to a narrow width, or one that's mounted on hinges to provide a game table or, in the case of a studio apartment, a dining table. A student desk or a modular unit designed to hold computer equipment can also be incorporated into a do-it-yourself wall unit.

To plan your own wall unit, first measure the wall and the main components (such as the desk, table, or chest of drawers). Then draw out a "design" on paper, making sure you allow enough space between all of the shelves for head room, or to hold necessary equipment, books, sculptures, records, and the like. You can get materials from the un-painted furniture store (good for chests and small desks), from furniture or office supply stores (good for computer stands), and from the lumber or building supply store (good for wood for shelving, and the standards and brackets for mounting the shelves). You can stain or paint the unit to fit your decor, while still maintaining a high degree of organizational usefulness. Also remember that you can design any wall unit around special paintings or large framed photographs for a decorative effect.

Don't forget window seat possibilities — they offer storage and a pleasant place to relax and read or play a game. You can have one built for you, or you can probably adapt a small cabinet, purchased from the unpainted furniture store for the purpose. These units are usually stacked as a part of a wall unit; for a window seat, simply use one or two of these units next to each other, painted or stained, and topped with cushions of your choice.

Magazine racks do a good job of at least keeping magazines in one place; a cloth organizer that hangs over your favorite chair will hold the *TV Guide* and TV remotes. Some ottomans are designed to hold craft supplies such as knitting yarn and needles, and if little children use the room frequently, keep a rolling toy cart in a corner so that the toys can be consolidated and out of the way when not in use.

Entertainment Centers

Much of the activity that goes on in the living room centers around the television and/or stereo equipment. Special cabinetry can consolidate all of the equipment and save overall space in the room. These units will hold the

This wall unit is actually three units placed together to serve as a compact entertainment center with several shelves that are perfect to display decorative items. Acknowledgment: O'Sullivan's Industries.

television, VCR, and/or stereo turntable, amplifier, and speakers. You can put your equipment on one of these freestanding units, or you could convert an antique armoire to do the job. You can also place the various components at strategic spots on your floor-to-ceiling wall unit. If you have more tapes and/or records than the unit will accommodate, you can store them in an antique buffet, modern credenza, or on open shelving (on your floor-to-ceiling wall unit). Pull-out racks can be helpful for storing cassette and videotapes, and can be placed on shelves in cabinets, reducing the piles of tapes that inevitably result when they are stacked on any shelf.

Books

If books are stored in the living room, a floor-to-ceiling wall unit will keep them organized all in one place, or you can use smaller bookcases in different areas of the room. They can be backed against the sofa, or at the ends of the sofa, with the top of the bookcase serving as space for a lamp, magazines, and the like. These smaller bookcases will also often fit into odd spaces in the room (such as the space between the heater and a corner, or under a window). If you've got more books than room, your spare room may be the answer. If you don't have a spare room, give some books away before they run you out of house and home.

A studio apartment can benefit from this storage arrangement, which turns one room into a living room, dining room, and storage area. Acknowledgment: Techline, by Marshall Erdman & Associates, Madison, Wisconsin. Photo by Steven Rhyner.

Chapter 3:
Dining Room

Although the dining room was originally intended as a room for *dining*, more often than not, it is used for this purpose only on special occasions. Instead the family eats in the kitchen, breakfast nook, or even in the living room on TV trays. Meanwhile, the dining room space either goes to waste or is not used as effectively as it could be. However, in some dining rooms there is room for a china hutch, buffet, or sideboard which can be used to store not only fine china and silver, but anything else you need to find a home for. Closed dining room storage such as buffets, which are really just cabinets with shelves and usually some drawers, can be used to hold art supplies, office supplies, out-of-season sweaters, cassette and videotapes, and anything else that you need stored behind closed doors. Hutches with glass doors can house books, knick-knacks, and collections as well as fine glassware and china. Space permitting, you can even put up a wall unit in the dining room that can hold glassware and liquor, making it an instant "bar." Plants, photos, and other mementos can be displayed on the upper shelves.

Storing things other than china, silver, and glassware, in these hutches and buffets works best when the room is multifunctional. For example, if you regularly do paperwork at the table, it makes perfect sense to have your paper supplies immediately at hand. Or, if you work on art projects here (perhaps with a drop cloth over the table), you'll want the art supplies close at hand. On the other hand, if you're experiencing a real storage space crunch, you may want to adapt this advice, storing things here even if they are used in another room. For instance, you could use the buffet as an instant linen cabinet if you have no linen closet.

Small apartments or condominiums that have a combined living and dining room can use bookcases to serve as a partial divider between the two spaces. If there is room you can place two bookcases back to back, with the bookcase facing the dining area used to store glassware, and the bookcase facing the living area used to store books. For extremely small studio apartments where there is virtually no space allocated for dining, a wall unit running the length of the studio can be the answer. A drop-down table, mounted on hinges, can be built into the wall unit design, so that it can be pulled into position as for meals. (It also functions as work space for writing or paying bills.) If you entertain, there are freestanding tables today that fold down to occupy only inches of space, yet can be extended to seat six. Or a Parsons table could double as a desk and be cleared to seat several people for dinner in a too small studio apartment.

Other storage possibilities in the dining area include a small attractive dresser or a nightstand with drawers that can be used to hold placemats and napkins along with special candles. You could install a custom wine rack in the dining room, either along a wall or as a

14 *This closet has been converted into a bar and wine storage area.*
Acknowledgment: Design by Kathleen Poer, Spacial Design; photograph by Vera Topinka.

divider between the dining and living areas, or you might use a freestanding rack that's mounted on the wall, or placed along a short wall or in a corner.

If your dining room does double duty as a hobby center or office, how about running closed cabinetry around the room? This can be as simple as getting unfinished wood cupboards or as fancy as ordering custom-built cabinets. Low cabinetry can be topped with cushions to provide a seating area for reading or other activities, and, with the table pulled over, it serves as the seating for dining as well. And, although traditionally the table sits in the center of the dining room, if you need more functional space, experiment with plac-

ing the table against a wall to free u wall space in the room for storage. If y the entire table for dining (to seat four people every day), you might be able to p the table with the short end against the wall (losing only one seat), then lift up one of the end leaves to compensate. By pushing even one end against the wall you can often buy lots of extra space in the dining room and unclog traffic as well.

Remember that just because it is the "dining" room doesn't mean that you have to stick to tradition and use it only for that purpose. The dining area represents space, and where there's space, there's storage potential to serve just about any possible need.

This cabinetry can accommodate any number of things. Here, one side has been turned into a bar, and the other side has been utilized as an entertainment center. China, silver, and table linens could also be easily stored, or if you use your dining room table for paperwork, this cabinet will do a nice job storing office supplies. Acknowledgment: Wood-Mode Cabinetry.

16

This cabinetry is integrated into the design of the kitchen with the built-in appliances and refrigerator strategically positioned. The island range and breakfast bar invite conversation and function to meet in the "heart" of the home. Acknowledgment: Ellipse Deluxe, Rutt Custom Kitchens.

Chapter 4:
Kitchen

When we think of the kitchen, all sorts of fantasies come to mind: soup simmering on the stove, bread baking in the oven, and a cherry pie cooling on the windowsill; family breakfasts à la "Father Knows Best," with stacks of perfectly formed pancakes served to beaming, well behaved children and a happy husband, complete the fantasy. Everything is mysteriously but perfectly stored in some miraculous place, where the happy cook can reach anything s/he wants in a flash.

Reality, alas, presents another picture altogether. More often than not, the storage and counter space seems to evaporate until there's very little, if any work space, and the storage space is woefully inadequate to contain the kitchen paraphernalia that may or may not get used by the chief cook and bottle washer.

Traffic in the kitchen also affects the efficiency of the room. If the back door leads into the kitchen, the kitchen table can actually add to the chaos as it, too, becomes a storage drop spot. If the family tends to come into the house through the back door, you might want to set up a rolling basket system for family members to drop their paraphernalia when they come in the back door. These systems contain several baskets so that each family member can claim a basket of his or her own (label the baskets to avoid confusion). This personal basket system provides a place for everyone to drop their gear—from mittens to schoolwork to keys. It takes up minimal space

and can be placed near the door (its portability leaves placement up to you—base your decision on the traffic). The kitchen table can then be used as extra work space if you are short of counter space, and it can then serve its original purpose as a dining table for family meals or quiet cups of coffee over the morning paper. If there's simply no room for this basket system, you can at least tackle part of the problem with hooks, a mug rack, or a pegboard system, that family members can use for anything that is hangable, such as keys and handbags.

This tilt-out sink tray uses space that otherwise be ignored. Acknowledgment: Cabinets by Merillat, "America's Cabinetmaker."

Many people like to carve out a corner in the kitchen for paperwork—menu planning, family scheduling, and/or bill paying. This seems like a good idea at first, until bits and pieces of paper start to infiltrate other areas of the kitchen, often to be lost or buried in piles of mail or notes.

A small kitchen office works only so long as you limit what goes on there (remember, a kitchen is not really an office). Menu planning and a calendar with the family's schedule can easily be accommodated, but once you start paying family accounts and trying to keep other financial or personal records in that small area, you may find you need more storage space than you have. Shelves on the wall can be helpful, as can rolling wire file bins that can be pulled over to the work area. But once that allocated storage is used, rather than let the paperwork spread to other parts of the kitchen, look for an area in another part of the house that can be turned into a small home "office." For instance, a desk and a two-drawer filing cabinet in a bedroom or family room nook, the dining room, or even the laundry area could be an alternate solution for domestic paper processing and storage.

What is the purpose of your kitchen? As-

Kitchen cabinets can be outfitted with accessories to handle almost any type of storage requirements. Here pull-out and round-table shelving makes everything in the kitchen easy to store and retrieve. Other space-saving features include the knife rack, cookbook holder, and spice rack that are mounted under the upper cabinets and folded up when not in use. Acknowledgment: Keije® cabinet organizer system by Clairson International.

suming that the purpose is to prepare and/or serve food in that room, you'll want to evaluate how the room is used now and eliminate anything that is being stored there—either temporarily or permanently—that doesn't have to do with food. Once you've done that, go through everything else, keeping only what you need and actually use on a regular basis. Next, store those items close to their point of use. Rarely used items (such as the turkey platter) can be stored in upper cabinets or at the back of very deep lower cabinets. For example, if you rarely bake, there's no need to keep the baking pans in the front of the pots and pans cabinet; but if you love baking, you'll want to establish a "baking center" with all of your baking pans and accessories in one storage area as close to the oven as possible.

the refrigerator. You can also give yourself a small piece of instant temporary work space by placing a cutting board over an open drawer or over the sink. (Manufacturers even offer special sink-top models.) Or you might want to put a work station near the area where you need the extra counter space. These work stations can be portable (equipped with casters, they are also sometimes called kitchen centers), so that they can be moved as needed. If you need more counter space near the stove when cooking, move it closer to the stove; if you need more space daily next to the refrigerator, position the work station there. These units also afford extra storage space for everything from cookbooks to appliances, cookware, or kitchen linens.

This island serves several purposes, providing both countertop and storage space. Acknowledgment: Techline by Marshall Erdman & Associates, Madison, Wisconsin. Photo by Steven Rhyner.

Counter Space

If you lack counter space, you can give yourself instant extra space by installing a shelf (either stationary or one that folds down when not in use) on the wall next to (for example)

If you are short of storage space for cookware or appliances, a cart can give you extra space for those items and provide more room for food preparation as well. Acknowledgment: Photograph courtesy of Pottery Barn Catalogue.

Space permitting, islands, which are fixed and larger than the portable work station, can also offer extra counter space as well as substantial storage underneath the worktop area. This storage area can be ideal for baking or casserole dishes, or can serve as a home for appliances that are not used on a daily basis. If the kitchen floorplan allows it, extra dining space can be added to the kitchen for eating and snacking simply by running a counter around at least one side of the island to create an eating nook, with stools for seating.

Appliances

In our quest for labor and time-saving devices, we often grab for the newest fandangled gadget on the market, and once it comes home to the kitchen, we have a hard time figuring out where to put the thing. Many are more complicated than anticipated, most require electricity, and all need storage space as well as work space for when the appliance is actually being used. Unfortunately, the average kitchen has a shortage of outlets, counter or work space, and storage space—all needed for the care and feeding of our appliances. Because of this, one by one, the appliances get stuffed into the back of the deepest kitchen cabinets, rarely to be retrieved because, on the rare occasions that you need the thing, it's just too much trouble to dig it out and put it away again.

Reevaluate your appliances, and give those almost never used ones to charity. Now is also the time to deal realistically with broken appliances. Either get it fixed so you can use it, or send it to a charity that repairs items for resale to benefit their cause.

Appliances that you use regularly (such as the coffee pot) can be put on the counter or on a portable kitchen center (look for the centers that feature electrical outlet strips so you can store and operate more than one appliance on the center). Some manufacturers now make appliances such as coffeemakers, toasters, and can openers that can be mounted under wall cabinets, so your countertops remain clear for other food preparation activities.

Another way to free up counterspace is to use appliances that can be permanently mounted on the upper cabinetry. Acknowledgment: Courtesy Black & Decker.

Miscellaneous attachments and parts should be matched up with the correct appliance, and if possible, be kept near that appliance (you can get a rack or hanging pocket holder for food processor blades, for example, and these could be stored in a cabinet near the processor, rather than putting the blades dangerously into the utensil drawers). If you have a substantial number of appliance cords and attachments, store them in a drawer by themselves, or in a labeled box in the cabinet.

Pantries, Cupboards, and Shelves

Although pantries and cupboards initially seem to offer enough storage space in the kitchen, often they are inadequate as things get shoved into back areas to be lost and forgotten, while new things vie for what little space is available in front. One of the best solutions to this problem is to restructure the interior storage so that everything that's stored there can always be brought into full view. This also makes it easier to keep cupboards and shelves clean, and can save time when you're trying to put a meal together in a hurry.

Another solution is to add shelves in areas you hadn't previously considered, such as a small shelf directly under an upper cabinet. Or sometimes you can double your current interior shelf space by adding another shelf in areas where shelves are traditionally too far apart. Turntables and other organizers can add the final space-saving touches to this valuable interior storage space.

Canned Goods and Staples

Canned goods are usually stored in either a pantry or in a cupboard that has been allocated for that purpose (next to, say, the pots and pans cupboard). If you are contemplating a complete renovation of your kitchen cabinetry, consider the wide variety of custom swing-out cabinetry now available. These designs will store more than the average cupboard or pantry shelf; with a touch, they bring the items into full view, providing easy retrieval and storage.

If you are not customizing your cabinet in-

teriors, you can still give yourself more storage space with over-the-door racks, turntables (these will only work with lightweight items), and shelf extenders. Check your shelves for depth and height, since often the simple addition of a shelf can make all the difference. Try a graduated shelf in a too deep cabinet or install a second shelf in a cabinet that has double the height necessary for canned goods. Not only do these additions bring the food into view, they make retrieving

You can give yourself instant extra shelf space with these handy clip-on wire baskets. Acknowledgment: Lillian Vernon Catalogue.

21

and putting the items away a simple, efficient task.

Staple ingredients do best if they are put in containers before being stored in the drawers or cabinets. The containers will save space, and also keep bugs out of things like flour and corn meal. Manufacturers of food storage dishes have started making modular see-through containers that are perfect for cereal, flour, sugar, and the like. They can be stacked easily, and make the most of whatever shelf space you have, particularly since you can stack a combination of tall and small sizes to make use of the extra height between some cabinet shelves. Potatoes and onions might be stored in stacking or rolling bins, baskets, or drawers. Hanging vegetable baskets could also accommodate small fruits and vegetables attractively out in the open where they are easy to get to. Odd-shaped corner cabinets with very little real storage will often hold a bin, basket, or small round trash can to accommodate potatoes and the like.

As you carve out these special food storage areas, remember to put the foods as close to their point of first use as possible. Ideally, cereal should be located near the cereal bowls, potatoes and onions should be near the sink for peeling, pasta near the stove, and flour and sugar near the oven or baking center. It's not always possible to put every food item next to where it is used (canned goods often are in a pantry that may not really be near the stove), but wherever possible, and especially for items used in everyday cooking and eating, if you can design your storage setup to match your work areas, you'll save yourself steps and make preparing food a much more pleasant experience.

Dishes

Many people have enough dishes hidden behind cabinet and hutch doors to outfit an army. If there are four people who normally eat meals at your house, two complete sets of dishes for twelve, thirty-six assorted glasses, and who knows how many mugs, are more than you will ever need. Select one set of dishes to use every day and store them near the dishwasher so that they are easy to put away after cleanup. Glasses should be near the sink if possible, and ideally, the coffeepot should be placed near the cabinet that holds the coffee cups.

These instant bag and wrap organizers can be mounted inside a cabinet or pantry door or on a wall in the kitchen for easy access and simple storage. Acknowledgment: Rubbermaid's Wrap and Bag Organizers.

Shelving and swing-out units can be put to efficient use in the pantry, nearly doubling the storage capacity in this area. Acknowledgment: Cabinets by Merillat, "America's Cabinetmaker."

23

You can increase your storage space for your dishes by installing cup hooks inside the cabinets as well as underneath the cabinets. Consider installing just a few hooks under the top cabinet near the coffeepot for hanging mugs—they'll be easy to grab for coffee, and you'll have more space inside the cupboard for the other dishes. Or add a shelf inside the cabinet (you can buy instant shelves that require no carpentry for installation), and put plate racks in the cabinet to maximize the storage capacity. Good dishes that are not used very often can be stored on upper shelves, and if you want to spare yourself the chore of washing all of them before you use them, your best bet is to store them in quilted or plastic dish caddies inside the cupboard.

Utensils and Gourmet Gadgets

Kitchen utensils multiply mercilessly until there are drawers full of spatulas, can openers, wooden spoons, wire whisks, spaghetti twirlers, pastry blenders, egg beaters, corn-on-the-cob holders, meat thermometers, and dozens of whatchamacallits and assorted thingamajigs. To make matters worse, duplicates pop up all over the place; appliance parts that you suspect (but don't know for certain) belong to the blender, food processor, and/or pressure cooker complete the mess.

To counteract this proliferation and open up some immediate storage space, first get rid of unnecessary duplicates and other utensils that you never use. With the purpose of the kitchen (preparing and eating food) fixed firmly in mind, go through your flatware and clear out anything that does not actively contribute to the business of daily cooking and eating. Unless you have dozens of family members chowing down at your place every day, you won't need three sets of flatware. Pick what you'll need and use and store it in a cutlery tray in a drawer near the dishwasher or the sink.

Cooking utensils can be stored either in drawers, containers, or on wall-mounted racks, pegboard systems, and grids. When you are selecting a storage method remember to keep items as close to their functional area as possible. Keep knives near the cutting board and cooking utensils near the stove. Rarely used items (like the turkey baster) can be stored in out-of-the-way drawers or cabinet spaces for retrieval on the few occasions that you use them. Utensils that are used regularly can be stored in drawers with dividers or cutlery trays. Knives can be stored (with caution, especially if you have children) in a knife block on the counter near the stove, or on the kitchen work center or island. Another option is a wall mounted magnetic strip knife rack placed near the cutting board. Often used wooden spoons and the like can be stored upright in a ceramic jar either on or adjacent to the stove or work area. Many utensils such as spatulas and large turning forks have a hole in the handle so they can be hung on hooks, pegs, or pegboard or grid systems on the wall. If you only hang what you use regularly, there will be no need to worry about the utensils getting dirty since they will be washed so often that there won't be any dirt or grease build up.

Once you've cleared out the clutter and creatively organized and stored the remaining utensils, remember that in the future, unless you are the world's most accomplished cook, you won't need to increase your utensil inven-

Making use of wall space over the counter can free up more counterspace for food preparation. Here wall-mounted dry food storage, utensil organization, and paper towel and waxed paper holders free up not only counterspace, but drawer and cabinet space as well. Acknowledgment: Rosti (USA) Inc.

Pots, pans, and baking equipment can be
more organized and accessible when stored
on these pull-out storage trays. Acknowledgment: Cabinets by Merillat, "America's Cabinetmaker."

tory beyond the basics that you already have on hand. After all, Grandma was a great cook, and she didn't have all of those utensils and gadgets, so why should you?

Pots and Pans

There's never enough storage space in the kitchen, it seems, for the pots and pans. They're stacked in an unmanageable heap (sometimes alongside small appliances) on the one or two available shelves in the lower cabinets. To make the best use of the storage space available for not only the pots and pans, but also the bakeware, casserole dishes, and mixing bowls, first, get rid of all of the old pots and pans that you never use. Remaining special trays, molds, and pans that get used only at holiday time should be moved to the hinterlands, such as the cabinet over the refrigerator or stove. This storage space can be increased by adding shelves either horizontally, or vertically. Trays and flat pans can then be stored, divided by the shelves, one or two at a time. This puts an end to storing those items in ever collapsing piles. (You could also turn the cabinet over the refrigerator into a wine storage rack by installing dividing shelves designed to hold the bottles.) Check odd-shaped and corner cabinets for possible storage or unusual or rarely used items as well; these spaces can often be customized to hold trays, bakeware, or other pots and pans (such as that stew pot) that could use their own special storage niche.

You can make storing your remaining everyday pots and pans and other bake and cookware less aggravating by installing pull-out shelves in the cabinet which insures that the equipment is easy to get to and put away.

Another option is to hang the pots from a ceiling pot rack, or from a pegboard or grid and hook system near the stove. Or you could hang your pots and pans inside the pantry door, providing there is enough clearance between the pots and the shelves, and so long as the door is thick enough to accommodate the hooks.

Recipes and Cookbooks

Recipes come into the kitchen via magazines, newspapers, friends, relatives, and cookbooks. Cookbooks are easy to deal with so long as you buy and keep only those cookbooks that you intend to use, and store them on a shelf rather than on the counter where they just get in the way. Watch the weight of these books; if you mount a shelf on the wall to hold them, it will need to be sturdy, or you'll risk having it pull down from the weight of the books. If you have too many cookbooks to store in the kitchen, put the excess on a bookshelf elsewhere in the house, or better yet, photocopy your favorite recipes and give the books away.

The other recipes aren't quite so simple. Recipes clipped from magazines and newspapers commingle with those time-honored, much-loved recipes from Grandma and your mother-in-law. Rarely do these recipes get used, since digging through the piles of clippings is almost always too time consuming to be considered; they just take up valuable kitchen storage space. To reverse this storage sapping trend, you'll need to follow the first rule of recipes which is that unless you are going to put your clipped recipes in order, and follow up by actually using those recipes on a reasonably regular basis, *don't clip them in the first place.* Because if you do, that one bulging drawer of yellowing, never-used recipes will multiply to fill two or three drawers that you could be using to store something else that you actually *use.*

For those recipes that you *do* want to use, you make your own personal cookbook that you can store on the shelf with the others. Simply enclose recipes in plastic sheet protectors (available at stationery stores) and put them in a three-ring binder by category (i.e., entrees, desserts, soups, etc.). This binder makes it easy to keep the photos of the recipe with the recipe—even if you have to use two pages. Simply put the picture in a sheet protector, and put it in the binder to the left of the recipe. Your customized cookbook can be expanded or weeded out at any time, and will be easy to keep clean. It's simple to add recipes to the proper category, and if you wish, you can snap one of the sheet protector recipes out of the binder and work from that one easy-to-clean page, eliminating the need to have bulky books on the counter while you are cooking. If your recipe collection is extensive, you might want to have separate binders for separate categories. This book takes care of all recipes, whether they're on scraps of paper or an entire magazine page, and, when shelved, can open up substantial drawer space in your kitchen.

Spices

Spices clutter up the cupboards with small and large tins and bottles vying for what little space there is in the first place. Cooks in a hurry tend to put the spices that are most often used in the front, and conveniently forget everything behind the front row. If you haven't used a particular spice for a long time, and can't think when you will, get rid of it.

Spices that are kept and used regularly should be stored either alphabetically or by category (in groups like baking spices, herbs,

This drawer has been fitted with a spice tray insert to keep spices neatly organized near their first point of use—the stove. Acknowledgment: Cabinets by Merillat, "America's Cabinetmaker."

curry spices, etc.). You can put them on turntables in the cupboard nearest the stove, or you can install a narrow shelf under your upper cabinets, over the counter. Since spices require minimal depth for storage, this shouldn't interfere with your counter space. You can also install a shelf or two on the wall near the stove. If you purchase a spice rack, either wire or wood, it should accommodate round glass jars as well as oblong tins (if you use them). Another solution is to turn a drawer near the stove into a spice section. This is done by making a step-like insert and putting it into the drawer. The spices are then laid into the drawer, with the steps providing support and division for the spices. Other options include a flat rack that mounts under the upper cabinet and folds down when you need it, or a door rack on the front or back of the pantry door.

Cleaning Supplies

The kitchen often houses the cleaning supplies, particularly for apartment dwellers. But whether you live in an apartment or a house, you need to take a look at the supplies you

This undersink roll-out can organize the cleaning clutter typically stored under the kitchen sink and can put an end to knocking over bottles and cans to get to the supplies at the back of the cabinet. Acknowledgment: Lillian Vernon Catalogue.

stock before you deal with the issue of storing those supplies. Too often people run out and buy the latest fancy cleanser, which never gets used because nobody wants to cart a zillion bottles and cans all over the house to do something as simple as *clean.* The cleansers get shoved into the far reaches of the kitchen cabinet under the sink where they are ultimately forgotten. So if you've got a lot of gourmet cleaning products that you never use, you might want to think about giving them to someone who wants to spend more of their time cleaning than you do. Stock the basics — cleaners that will do double, or even triple, duty for you. These can be stored in an under-sink pull-out storage rack, or on lazy Susans in the cabinet. Access is simple, and you'll eliminate the knock-the-bottles-in-the-front-to-get-to-the-bottles-in-the-back problem. Basic cleaning supplies might also be stored in a cleaning caddy which can then be carried from room to room when cleaning. To child-proof the supplies, put them in a caddy or dish-pan and store them on an upper cabinet shelf.

Brooms, mops, dustpans, and even buckets can be hung on wall space with clamps or hooks. Wall space in the pantry, broom closet, next to the refrigerator, or at the top of the cellar stairs can hold some, or all, of these items. Depending on the location, you might even be able to install a shelf on the same wall space to hold supplies, or you can hang an over-the-door rack to store your supplies. The rack can go on the back of or inside of, a door either in, or near, your kitchen.

However you store and organize your cleaning supplies, try to remember that the more supplies you have on hand, the more work it is to clean. In addition to the cleaning, you have to keep organizing and cleaning the cleaning supply storage area — a chore that the average clean person could live happily ever after without. Since it's unrealistic to eliminate cleaning altogether, the next best thing is to cut back on the process and paraphernalia used for those chores. Not only will you save storage space, you'll save time otherwise spent cleaning.

Tips from the Pros

Greg Wolf, Merillat Industries, Inc.

"The kitchen truly is the heart of the home," says Greg Wolf, Director of Product Planning at Merillat Industries, Inc. in Adrian, Michigan. Merillat is the nation's leading manufacturer of cabinetry for the kitchen, bath, and home, with distributors nationwide. Before Merillat introduces a new line of cabinetry, Wolf analyzes and studies design, manufacturing, and retail trends in the industry so that each design selected provides the homeowner with cabinetry that will add to the design as well as the function of their storage space in any area. He also works with cabinet accessories which he says can make a major contribution to an efficient kitchen. According to Wolf, you can "customize" your new kitchen by installing cabinet interior and decorative accessories to maximize the storage capacity to suit your specific needs in the kitchen. These are some of the possibilities for accessorizing your cabinetry:

• **Pantry Cabinet.** Shelving, and swing-out units can be put to efficient use in the pantry, nearly doubling the storage capacity in this area. For example, a thirty-six-inch-wide pantry can provide up to thirty-two cubic feet of storage by utilizing shelf space, movable swing units, and interior door space.

• **Revolving Shelves.** These turning shelves can fit into any number of cabinet areas, providing easy visual access to the contents within. You can virtually insure that no space is left unturned or unused with these units which can fit snugly into a corner cabinet or other cabinets, providing fingertip access to kitchen storage space.

• **Cutting Board.** You can conveniently prepare vegetables and fruits on a cutting board which slides beneath the counter for storage when not in use.

• **Knife Tray.** A pull-out knife tray organizes and safely stores knives.

• **Drawer Dividers.** When you order the cabinetry, don't forget to order some divided drawers to keep your silverware and cutlery organized.

• **Appliance Garage.** You can turn a corner or other countertop area into an appliance "garage" by installing a pull-down "door" to keep toasters, mixers, and other appliances out of sight.

• **Microwave Oven Cabinets.** You can free up countertop space by installing a special shelf above the counter to hold the microwave.

• **Bread Box.** A kitchen drawer can be turned into a bread box by installing this accessory, which is a bright metal box with a sliding top that helps keep bread and bakery goods fresh.

• **Cookware Pull-Outs.** Your pots and pans can be made more accessible if you install these shallow pull-outs in your lower cabinets. Instead of digging to get at the cookware in the back, you can simply pull all of the items into view for easy selection any time.

• **Decorative Shelving.** If you want to add an extra decorative touch to the kitchen, you can order shelves to match the cabinetry that can be mounted either on the wall or on cabinetry that is attached to the floor (such as the kitchen island extension). These small shelves can be used to display flowers, dinnerware, cookbooks or knickknacks, providing a personal touch to your kitchen.

32

Pantry-like cabinets can be put to good use in the laundry area. Here, a wire bin mounted on the door holds laundry, and racks and hooks hold cleaning supplies. A rod mounted next to the washer/dryer provides a place to hang clothes that have just been ironed or are fresh out of the dryer. Acknowledgment: Wood-Mode Cabinetry.

Chapter 5:
Laundry Area

Laundry areas are often carved out of basement or garage space, or are squeezed into a small area generally located near the kitchen and/or back door. Since the laundry facilities are used on a regular basis, it is important to keep the area clear of clutter. Your first step is to firmly establish that this area is for the laundry *only*, regardless of where that area is. In the garage, let everyone know that tools do not belong on top of the washer; in the basement make it clear that the catcher's mitt and bat do not belong on the washer/dryer, and if the area is near the kitchen or back door, it is important to let everyone know that the washer and dryer are not there to serve as a dumping ground as people pass by.

That established, check the surrounding wall space above the washer/dryer, and next to it as well. Shelving can often be installed in these areas to hold laundry supplies. (If you have young children make sure you store toxic cleaning substances in a cabinet with doors that can be locked, or on a high shelf.) If you have room next to the washer/dryer, install shelving that leaves room at the bottom (say waist high) for some clothing bins. Space permitting, you might want to keep large bins or baskets in the laundry area to sort the laundry into darks, whites, lights, hand washables, etc. If you have a large family, consider installing shelves that will hold bins or wire baskets—one for each member of the family. If you don't have the wall space, a couple of rolling basket systems will do just as well. As you fold the dry clothes, put them into the labeled basket for each member of the family. They can then retrieve their clean clothes from the laundry area on their own and put them away in their rooms. In connection with this, you could have a dirty clothes receptacle in each bedroom as well as in the bathroom. On wash day, everyone simply brings his or her load to the laundry room. A separate container for dry cleaning might also be handy.

It's also a good idea to have a small container in the laundry area to hold all of the miscellaneous things that are pulled from pockets before laundering the clothing. And don't forget to keep a trash basket nearby to collect the empty soap boxes, lint, and other trash that seems to accumulate here. If you have the space, either a laundry basket or a basket within a custom-installed system or rolling basket system, can be set aside for items that are ill-fitting, out of date, or just plain not wanted any more. Toss those unwanted clothes into the designated bin, and when the bin is full, give it all away to your favorite charity. This eliminates clutter not only in the laundry room, but also in closets—where outgrown and unwanted clothes are often responsible for a good portion of the cramming that occurs.

A portable rack to hang clothing on when it comes out of the dryer helps keep things organized and saves future ironing time as well.

This laundry room storage packs a lot into a confined space. A roll-out holds cleaning supplies and the iron under the portable ironing board, and other drawers and bins hold light tools and hardware, dirty clothes, and other miscellaneous things. The countertop over the storage is perfect for folding clothes out of the dryer. Acknowledgment: Wood-Mode Cabinetry.

Hang up to-be-ironed items immediately (keep a supply of hangers in the laundry area) then transfer them to the rack. If you don't have room for a freestanding rack, you can get an over-the-door rack or a rack that can be mounted directly onto the wall—both of which will hold several articles of clothing. For flat clothes that need to be ironed, a basket or bin kept near the hanging rack serves nicely.

The ironing board and iron can be installed on the wall or in the utility cupboard, or on the back door with a rack designed for that purpose. Or, you can do what used to be common practice—install a small ironing board that is concealed in a cabinet or mounted di-

rectly to the wall and folds out when you need it and drops flat when you don't.

Finally, if you have the space, keep a table near the washer/dryer for folding clean clothes (you can keep the basket that holds outgrown clothes underneath). If there isn't room for a table, you can mount a drop-down shelf on the wall; when not in use, simply fold it up.

This easy-to-install rack can hold ironing equipment on a wall or in a pantry near the laundry room. Acknowledgment: Selfix, Inc.

Tips from the Pros
Judith Miley, *CHOISE* Clairson International

Judith Miley is the Executive Director and co-founder of CHOISE, the Center for Home Organization and Interior Space Efficiency. CHOISE is a nonprofit organization of architects, designers, builders, professional organizers, home economists, manufacturers of space efficient products, and other home improvement planners. Miley is also the Communications Manager for Clairson International, manufacturer of CLOSET MAID® and KEIJE® home storage organizers. Miley provides design and equipment tips to help storage industry professionals and homeowners alike rethink and "respace" their homes. She sees accessibility and safety as prime considerations when planning for storage needs, and offers these guidelines to help you design storage that will make it possible for you to see what you need, remember where it is stored, and get to it safely:

- **Plan the Space to Match the Activities.** Storage should minimize the need for lifting while stooping, bending, or stretching; store the heaviest items between knee and shoulder height.

- **Store Things within a Bird's-eye View.** Use glide-out cabinet organizers in kitchens and bathrooms for better visibility and access to items stored in the back of the cabinets.

- **Make Every Inch Count.** Tier shelving at varying heights to avoid wasting space and to allow appropriate storage for odd-shaped items.

- **Use Hanging Space.** Allow vertical cabinet space for cookie tins, trays, and platters. Include vertical hanging space for mops, brooms, and vacuums in a separate area of the pantry or in utility rooms.

- **Add Storage with Mobility.** Use mobile storage pieces for versatility and safety. Storage serving carts can take heavy appliances from the utility room or pantry to the work area, then transport finished meals, hot casseroles and tableware to the table. These carts permit users to set the table and serve the meal in one trip, and to clear the table in one trip.

- **Use Stackables.** Consider a stackable washer/dryer to reduce bending and lifting and to allow more storage and folding area.

- **Consider Light and Ventilation Needs.** Plan for adequate lighting and ventilation in storage areas. Ventilated storage systems of coated wire enable users to see through upper shelves to locate possessions and allow light and air to pass between the shelves.

36

This traditionally styled cabinetry offers storage space that can accommodate everything from grooming accessories to linens, all in one room. Acknowledgment: Cabinets by Merillat, "America's Cabinetmaker."

Chapter 6:
Bathroom

The bathroom is the nerve center of the average household, yet it is often woefully underequipped to serve everyone's storage needs. Since so much time is spent in the bathroom every day, coming up with enough space for life's daily grooming essentials can be the key to making the bathroom a better place to be, allowing everyone who uses it a cleaner, faster, and much calmer approach to yet another day.

Cabinetry and Shelving

Bathrooms usually have areas that can be turned into storage with the simple addition of extra cabinetry (either freestanding or fixed) or shelves. The wall space over the toilet is a prime area for adding shelves, which can be installed with brackets directly onto the wall (you can use wood or glass shelving). You can also purchase freestanding wicker or color-coordinated shelving to put over the toilet which adds storage and a touch of decoration to the room. Other freestanding options include narrow units made of wood or laminate and units that are supported by tension rods. Check under the sink for other storage possibilities. If the area is not enclosed, you can enclose it yourself with a skirt, or have a sink cabinet installed. Check the wall at the back end of the tub; if it isn't tiled, you can install a cupboard or shelves to provide extra storage. If you have a large bathroom with lots of blank wall space, you could hire professionals to install custom cabinets, or you can buy wicker, wood, or metal chests, tables, or cabinets to use for extra space. Small shelves can be installed below or around the medicine chest and in corners, and extra shelves can often be added to the interior of existing cabinetry to increase and maximize the cabinet space that you already have.

Clothes

Dirty Clothes seem to call for a hamper that can be placed against the wall. If there's enough wall space, you can put shelving above the hamper for extra storage (many manufacturers have wicker and metal hampers with shelving to match in different colors). If you are short on wall space, consider a laundry bag made from attractive fabric that can be hung on a hook either on the wall or door. A bin or pull-out basket inside a cabinet is yet another solution to the dirty underwear dilemma.

Hooks on the back of the bathroom door provide the simplest answer to robe and nightwear storage. These can include small over-the-door hanging racks (you'll need hangers, but you can hang a lot of items this way); porcelain, metal, or wood hooks; or even wooden mug racks (from the dime store) can do a good job of holding the clean clothes you're going to wear, so you can avoid making a nude mad dash to another room for cover.

Cosmetics

Cosmetics often accumulate by the truckload, overrunning virtually everything else in the

This vanity cabinet is an adaptation of an original Chinese drawer chest. The elegant and detailed design of the front conceals interior shelving to accommodate cosmetics and other personal needs. Acknowledgment: Kohler Co.

bathroom. To conquer the cosmetic storage challenge and bring the bathroom storage space allocation up to more equitable standards, first get rid of anything that is old, sticky, melted, or otherwise too gooey for words.

Once you have weeded out the cosmetics, the next step is to maximize your current storage to keep your makeup as organized as possible within a minimum amount of space. Use small baskets, plastic, Lucite, or ceramic containers to hold and group small items such as makeup brushes and manicure equipment. Store these containers in a deep drawer, in a cabinet on a pull-out tray or bin, or, if the container is attractive, you might even want to display it in a vanity area (wherever you put your makeup on) in the bathroom.

If you have enough drawer space (perhaps you have a built-in vanity in your bathroom, with adjacent drawers), drawer dividers can separate and organize your cosmetics and can be as simple as dropping in cutlery trays or as customized as having a space planner design inserts for the drawers so that they are designed especially for your makeup. However you do it, you'll want to make certain that the inserts are easy to remove and clean.

Another option is to keep the cosmetics you use on a regular basis in a clear plastic zippered bag. The bag can be stored out of sight in a drawer, cabinet, or covered basket. If you don't have drawer or cabinet space, try a makeup bag that you can hang on the back of the door or on the inside of a cabinet door. With everything in one bag, it takes up a lot less space, and you won't have to search through bathroom drawers for the lipstick.

This functional, space-saving pull-out can be extended for practical use or concealed altogether within the cabinetry. Acknowledgment: Wood-Mode Cabinetry.

The key to success with this storage method is to put everything back into the bag immediately after use. When you travel, simply grab the bag and go.

If you have too much makeup to keep in one small bag, a tackle or art supply box will organize all manner of cosmetics and can be stored and transported easily. If you need even more than that, purchase a portable makeup cart. These rolling units usually have a mirror so that, if you pull a stool up to the unit, you can use it as an instant vanity and apply your makeup right there. (Check beauty supply stores for these carts.)

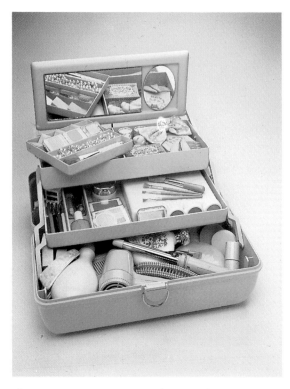

This cosmetics organizer can keep makeup contained for simple storage in a bathroom cabinet. Acknowledgment: Caboodles of California, a division of Plano Molding, Plano, Illinois.

Once you've reorganized your cosmetics, remember to eliminate old bacteria-laden items periodically. You'll find yourself with just what you need, when you need it, so that you can have a simple, time-saving start every day when you "put on your face."

Grooming Gear

Grooming gear runs the gamut from soaps to shaving creams to lotions and powders of all descriptions. These can be stored on lazy Susan turntables in the cabinets so that you won't have to keep knocking down bottles and cans in the front of the cabinet to get to those in the back. If you don't mind having items out, you can hang a shelf next to the sink where you can corral the items you use every day. There are racks and storage towers for the shower that will accommodate soap, shaving cream (for those who shave in the shower), and shampoos. Powders and potions that are attractively packaged can be stored on open shelving near the tub or sink, or near the vanity area (if you have one). Toothpaste and toothbrushes can be stored in a wall-mounted rack, or in individual cutlery trays in a drawer (the trays are easy to lift out for cleaning). Children can also have their own colored cup, with teeth-cleaning gear stored in the cup. Accessibility is the key to storing grooming aids. Anything that's used every day definitely needs to be within reach of where you use it, and in the bathroom, that usually means next to the tub or the sink.

Hair Paraphernalia

The tools that go into the care of one's crowning glory can require significant storage space. There are shampoos, conditioners, sprays,

41

This bath tower organizes bath and shower items where they are used in the shower or bathtub. Acknowledgment: Photograph courtesy of Hold Everything Catalogue.

hairbrushes and combs, clips and pins, ribbons and barrettes, and hair dryers, curling irons, and hot (and not so hot) rollers. One solution to storing this paraphernalia is to get it out of the bathroom altogether. For example, you could move this gear to a bedroom or even to a corner in the hall outside the bathroom. Put a small stand there for storage, hang an attractive mirror on the wall, and you've actually extended your bathroom.

If this isn't possible, look for storage solutions within the bathroom. Obviously, shampoos and conditioners belong where they are used — in the shower, stored on the shower caddy (mounted over the shower head), or in the caddy tower (mounted in the corner). Shelving next to the shower or tub will also hold these items. Sprays can be stored on turntables inside a cabinet, and clips, pins, and barrettes could be stored in a drawer with dividers, or in some stackable covered tins or baskets which might be placed either in the cabinet or on the vanity counter area. Special Lucite holders can be mounted on the wall or on the inside of a cabinet door to hold brushes, combs, hair dryers, and curling irons. Hot rollers need to be shelved inside a cabinet, and other rollers can be kept best in a bin (a simple small dishpan will do the trick if you have lots) on a shelf. Ribbons can be hung on a hook either on the wall or on the door or inside of a cabinet door.

Medicine

Medicine, including pills, tonics, creams, and sprays, should be kept, obviously, in the medicine chest. Today medicine chests often can't keep up with the supply which expands to include a staggering array of get-well items:

bandages, aspirin, cough syrup, pills, nose sprays, eye drops, face creams, lotions for rashes, past and present prescriptions, stomach stuff, and much, much more. You need to go over this oft-ignored area on a regular basis, weeding out old medicines, and long fossilized creams and potions. If you still need more room, you could perhaps buy another medicine chest and install it on another wall. Not only would you benefit from extra storage, but the additional mirror can mean that two people can gussy up at the same time in the bathroom rather than fighting for mirror time. If there is no wall space for another chest, you can put some of the items in a container, such as a covered basket or dishpan or kitty litter pan, and store them on a shelf in a cabinet (under the sink is another possible spot for these grouped medicines). If you have small children, it goes without saying that you will need to store these bins on a high shelf in a lockable cabinet.

Supplies

The most logical place to store bathroom supplies such as toilet paper, Kleenex, cleaning items, and backup cans and bottles of hair shampoos is under the sink. The cleaning items can be grouped in a caddy or on a turntable, and the other bottles and cans can also be stored in this manner. Toilet paper has traditionally been stuffed into whatever cabinet will accept it, but if ever there was a case to store something close to its point of use, toilet paper is the epitome of the seriousness of that concept. Get it as close to the toilet as you can, since somebody always takes the last of the paper without replacing it, leaving the next unsuspecting visitor to realize, often too

Every inch of space has been utilized to provide fingertip storage for things that need to be used on a regular basis. Acknowledgment: Wood-Mode Cabinetry.

late, that they are in a canoe without a paddle, so to speak. Other items such as soap and smaller supplies can be best stored in a drawer or covered basket. Or, if you've decided to incorporate a small "dressing" stand in the bathroom where you can keep your hairbrushes, etc., you might want to use a small cupboard or cabinet for this purpose. You can store extra supplies in the bottom part of the cabinet, and still have the countertop surface for your hairbrushes and clips.

43

If you simply can't store all of the supplies in the bathroom for lack of space, then you'll have to allocate some of your linen closet space to do the job. Depending on the amount of available space, you may want to keep your inventory of backup supplies down to an easily stored minimum, rather than having enough on hand to supply everyone on the block for the next six months.

Towels

People usually store their towels in the linen closet, but this is often not ideal. If your linen closet space is limited, you won't have enough room, particularly if the family goes through towels like Grant marching through Georgia; it can precipitate mad wet dashes into the hall to grab a towel. Since towels are often bright and attractive, and purchased with the bathroom color in mind, it can be fun to store a substantial supply in the bathroom on shelves (such as on shelving over the toilet). Towels can also be stored rolled in an attractive basket or flat in a wicker trunk or chest of drawers in the bathroom. Once the towel has been used, traditional towel racks as well as hooks can serve as temporary storage. Hooks and racks can be mounted nearly everywhere, on the door, walls, even on tiles in some cases (look for adhesive-backed hooks). A wooden mug rack on the back of the door will hold several towels (one peg per towel) while taking up a minimum of space. If you have children, be sure to mount hooks at child height so they can learn early on how to pick their towels up from the floor and hang them up.

Toys

Bath toys need to be kept in or around the tub so that children have them when they want them. On the other hand, adults shouldn't have to deal with squeaky toys when they're rushing to bathe and get out the door to work. Tub trays are one good compromise; these over-the-tub trays hold toys and can easily be moved out of the way when not needed. A hanging vegetable basket or a simple cotton mesh bag could also be hung on a hook to hold the rubber duckies and sailboats. If you can hang these within the tub enclosure, so much the better, since dripping toys will turn into dry toys in no time flat.

Tips from the Pros

Ellen Cheever, CKD, ASID National Kitchen & Bath Association

Author and marketing consultant Ellen Cheever is the Director of Special Projects for the National Kitchen and Bath Association in Hackettstown, New Jersey. Her textbook, *The Basics of Bathroom Design and Beyond*, is used in educational programs industry-wide. Her designs are known for both their practicality and imagination, and she presents her ideas and techniques in training programs at major industry conferences both domestically and internationally in Japan, Canada, New Zealand, and Australia. If you are thinking about redesigning your bathroom to include more storage, or if you are building a new bathroom, Cheever recommends that you follow these guidelines as you work with your bathroom designer:

- **Know What You Want.** Hold a family conference and make a list of what you dislike about your current bathroom and what your priorities are for the new bathroom. Your design will need to accommodate your budget, beauty, and function choices for the room.

- **Don't Be Afraid to Speak Up!** No professional—plumber or designer—can read your mind. Also, there is no perfect bathroom. The best solution will be the one that suits you and your family lifestyle. Therefore, if you never take a bath, but spend hours in the shower, let your planner know that.

- **Demystify the Plumbing System.** Select only a professional who is technically proficient and can talk to you. If you are doing something that involves moving or installing plumbing, remember that plumbers are great craftsmen who sometimes have difficulty verbally expressing their opinions, recommendations, or concerns. And, some designers are creative souls who know nothing about getting water to the fixtures! Select only professionals who can give you both a creative design and a working end product.

- **Understand the Plans Before You Okay Them.** Professional bath designers will go to great lengths to show you actual products in showrooms, detailed drawings, and exacting specifications. Make sure you understand what you are buying! Changes once the job starts are expensive.

- **Stay Flexible.** Once the project starts, cover up everything in the house of value, put on a pot of coffee for the workers, and settle in for a long, dusty, disruptive experience that includes unexpected delays. Remodeling is not an exact science. Just keep thinking of how beautiful the room will be when it is finished. Making sure that the workers have easy access to the area, keeping children and pets out of the construction zone, and providing garage space for product storage and trash collection will make the ordeal easier for everyone. A relaxed attitude and open mind on your part will make the experience less traumatic as you move toward your new bathroom with that much needed additional storage space.

46

The linen closet need not be used for linens. Here, a linen closet has been turned into a sewing center. Acknowledgment: Designs by Kathleen Poer, Spacial Design, photograph by David Wasserman.

Chapter 7:
Linen Closet

Linens, including towels and washcloths, tablecloths and napkins, sheets and pillowcases, blankets, and doilies made by your great-grandma, always seem like a necessity of daily life—and some of them are. Obviously towels and washcloths are put to good use every day, and bedding is also a daily linen necessity. But tablecloths, doilies, and linen napkins tend to be stored for special occasions, and in some cases those items are never actually used at all. Ultimately, the linens, good, bad, and daily, get piled into the linen cabinet to be pushed and shoved about as you struggle to get what you really need at any moment in time. The piles start to resemble towers, and invariably, the stacks of linens collapse into each other, leaving you to handle your mounting frustration as you try to locate a complete set of sheets for the children's bed or a clean towel for your dripping body.

To shorten the towers a bit, go through the linens and get rid of anything that can no longer be put to good use. Inherited items that you never use can be passed along to your heirs now to use in their homes. Raggedy sheets and towels that you really don't use can be turned into rags or tossed.

Adding Space

Once you've eliminated unnecessary linens, measure your linen closet and consider some storage and space-enhancing options. You could remove shelves from the bottom half of the closet, or, for that matter, turn the bottom of any closet into a linen closet by putting a basket system in that space. Linens are then divided and put in the baskets (which you can label), eliminating the piles and digging for the right sheets, washcloths, etc. To fix shelves with too much height between them (the primary cause of collapsing piles) simply install another shelf, perhaps an instant add-a-shelf (no carpentry needed). You can also hang clip-on wire baskets from the bottom of shelves to create some extra space for smaller items. Finally, go over everything in the closet and consider creative options for storing the items in other areas of the house (towels in the bathroom or sheets in various bedrooms, for example).

If you choose to organize your linen closet by moving things to other areas, you'll find yourself with some extra storage space that can be adapted to almost any purpose. You can store fabric and sewing supplies, craft supplies, toys and games, office supplies, or small sports gear in this newly found space. Now instead of a linen closet, you will have a storage center that will effectively hold the necessary accoutrements of one or more of your ongoing activities.

Blankets

Blankets are so bulky that they quickly eat up any closet space allocated to them. Consider storing them on a quilt rack or in a wicker trunk or cedar chest instead of in the linen closet; the trunk can double as a bedside stand or coffee table (simply put a piece of glass on it). Or you could keep blankets in a blanket box and store them under the bed or on a high closet shelf.

Out-of-season blankets can be stored in these underbed roll-out drawers. Acknowledgment: Photograph courtesy of Hold Everything Catalogue.

Doilies

If you don't have drawers in your linen closet, you can store these in a plastic sweater box or in a covered basket. They'll stay neater, and you'll be able to get a good look at them all whenever you want to select one to put out on the tables or chairs.

Do remember, though, that doilies were made to be used, and if you're not really using yours but you can't bear to part with them, they should be moved out of the active storage area and put away with other mementos and heirlooms.

Table Linens

Everyday placemats should be stored as close to the table as possible, either in the kitchen or dining room, and good placemats need to be stored flat on a high shelf or in a clip-on basket that only holds those items.

Special-occasion table linens need not be stored with the everyday linens. Set aside a special drawer for them or, if you have a basket system, a special basket. If you have no drawer, a plastic sweater box will hold small items such as napkins and keep them neatly pressed away from the other linens that are constantly shifted around. This box can be stored on a high shelf in the closet or in the buffet with your good dishes and silver, or, if you have exceptionally limited space, it can be stored on a shelf in the pantry or in a bedroom closet. Tablecloths are generally, because of their size, best stored flat, toward the bottom of the stack, or hung over a hanger. You can then hang them on a rod in the hall closet (if there's room) or on an over-the-door hanger in the hall or linen closet. Another option is to remove one or two shelves in the linen closet and install a short rod specifically to accommodate the space required for your tablecloths on hangers.

Sheets and Pillowcases

Extra shelves within your linen closet will make each stack of sheets and pillowcases smaller so that the linens don't end up in a collapsing pile. If you've got different-sized beds, mark the shelves with a label or a piece of tape (i.e., twin, queen), and when you put the sheets away, put them on the proper shelf. If you have a basket system, you can do the same, labeling the baskets to separate the sheets. When bedmaking time rolls around, whoever makes the bed can tell immediately which sheets to grab. If you are really short on linen storage space, consider storing the sheets on a closet shelf or in an underbed storage drawer in the bedroom where they're actually used.

Towels

Of all the linens, towels and washcloths are the simplest to store elsewhere. Extra shelving in the bathroom, a wicker trunk, or a nice basket to hold rolled towels in the bathroom can open up much needed space in your linen closet. If this is not feasible in your bathroom, be sure to add shelves to your linen closet since towels, like sheets, are prime candidates for a toppling pile incident. Washcloths can be segregated by putting them in a clip-on basket or drawer (either in the linen closet or in the bathroom). Dish towels should be kept in the kitchen if at all possible, if not, the clip-on basket or a shelf extender can make it possible to segregate these smaller towels from the other bulky towels so that you can grab one without any problem.

If you don't have a linen closet, you can turn an armoire into a linen storage center. Acknowledgment: Armstrong World Industries, Inc., Lancaster, Pennsylvania.

A bedroom with more than adequate storage
can be carved out of virtually any room in the
house. Acknowledgment: Techline by Marshall
Erdman & Associates, Madison, Wisconsin.

Chapter 8:
Bedroom

The phrase "behind closed doors" takes on special meaning when it comes to the master bedroom and the master bedroom closet. This room often serves more purposes than it was ever meant to serve, providing room for relaxation, intimacy, dressing, and storage. Some people further complicate the bedroom space issue by trying to fit office paraphernalia, exercise equipment, or craft supplies into the room. Clutter is magnetically attracted to dresser tops and the areas next to the bed. Magazines and paperback books commingle distressingly with nail polish, aspirin, and the alarm clock on the nightstand. Children and/or pets are forever passing through, and late-night snacks in bed can finish off the picture of a room stretched well beyond its capacity.

Cabinetry and Shelving

A good starting point for regaining control over the bedroom chaos is cabinetry and shelving. Built-in shelving surrounding the bed can provide organized storage space for books, cassettes, and magazines. Lighting can be incorporated into the design to provide reading illumination. A wall unit or entertainment unit does a good job of holding the TV, VCR, and any stereo equipment that might be in the room. If you have allocated space in the room for other purposes, such as crafts center or a small desk, make sure you contain that space with cabinetry or shelving concentrated in one area for storage of the supplies that go

with the activity. (It is preferable, however, to keep the bedroom separate from activities other than grooming, rest, or romance. Once you start using the room for lots of other activities, it's hard to retain the restful and romantic aspects of the room.)

As always, functional furniture will provide lots of space-saving storage. Armoires can be used for sweaters, exercise togs, linens, books and magazines, or to hold the TV and VCR. Entertainment centers, usually purchased for the living or family room, can also be used here in the bedroom for the television and/or stereo equipment. Or, you can install shelving on sturdy standards and brackets that are mounted directly onto the wall. Bedside tables with drawers, shelves, or closed cabinet fronts will hold books, magazines, and miscellaneous beauty paraphernalia that you might apply before bed (face cream or nail polish, applied while you watch TV, for example). A chest at the end of the bed can hold out-of-season sweaters or blankets; or you could top it with a piece of glass and use it as a bedside stand. Beds with built-in drawers can provide extra storage for linens or out-of-season clothes. Loft-type beds with built-in storage shelving or study areas are good for children's rooms or for studio apartments, and wall beds that fold up are good for guest rooms and too-small studio apartments.

Traditional dressers provide drawer space, but it may be preferable to rethink the closet space so that sweaters, tops, and shorts are

Nearly all of the furniture in the room provides functional storage space — the triple dresser, the armoire chest, the blanket chest at the foot of the bed, and the highboy chest of drawers. Even the nightstand has a drawer and a lower cabinet shelf for holding items. Acknowledgment: Armstrong World Industries, Inc., Lancaster, Pennsylvania.

folded on shelves rather than stuffed in dresser drawers, making it difficult to see what you want to get and impossible to keep the drawers neat. Dressers are probably best used for underwear, stockings, scarves, and the like, and a small dresser can very often be placed directly into the closet, saving overall floor space in the bedroom itself.

The Closet

The closet — whether it is a large walk-in or a small four-foot closet in an apartment bedroom — never seems adequate for the storage at hand. It all too quickly becomes stuffed: clothes, shoes, and accessories are crammed together with assorted other things that

This sleek cabinetry conceals a wealth of organized storage for clothing and other wardrobe accessories. Acknowledgment: Wood-Mode Cabinetry.

landed in that closet because there didn't seem to be anywhere else to put it all. Hangers get tangled up with plastic cleaner bags and with each other, and accessories such as belts and ties either fall on the floor or get caught in the rest of the mess.

To put an end to this cycle of clothes consternation, you will need to first empty your closet out so that you can organize what you have appropriately. Naturally you will be eliminating some things, which will mean that your shelving and organizational needs in the closet will probably be a bit different than what you may think you need now (now you think you need to move to larger quarters).

After you've taken everything out of the closet, set up four cartons labeled *charity, mending, elsewhere,* and *trash* (yes, trash—some clothes are in such bad shape that send-ing them to charity would be an insult). Tackle the mountain of clothes, one garment at a time, giving each careful consideration; does it really go back in the closet or does it belong in a carton? Remember that the *mending* carton is not supposed to be a holding bin that sits around indefinitely. Take those clothes to the seamstress or tailor *immediately*. Don't even consider doing them yourself. If those clothes have been waiting to be mended for months already and you haven't done it because you haven't had the time, you're not going to find the time to do it now. Put that box in the car at the end of your sorting/organizing session, along with the *charity* box, and drop them both off without delay.

What's In and What's Out

Deciding what to get rid of needn't be difficult.

Pull-out basket systems can be installed in any closet to suit your specific storage needs. Acknowledgment: Norscan® Scanimport America, Staten Island, New York.

Things that you know are the wrong color or "just not you" should go to charity or resale shops. Whoever you give the clothes to, the important thing is to get everything that's inappropriate *out of the closet* and *out of the house*, so you won't be tempted to put it back in the closet "just for now."

Things that are too small (and have been for quite some time), or are out of date, or that have been waiting to be altered for just about forever (and you are not going to get them altered) should also be given away. If it's far too big, or you never really liked it in the first place (you probably got it on sale), get rid of it. (If you still find yourself having a problem weeding things out of your closet, you might want to refer to my previous book, *How to Conquer Clutter*, for additional tips and inspiration.)

Hangables

As you put the good, fashionable clothes and accessories back into the closet, remember that your life (not to mention your storage needs) will be less complicated if you have a simple wardrobe that is comfortable, attractive, and interchangeable. Only keep clothes that you feel good wearing, and that you wear often.

Hang your clothes in the closet to see just where you stand in terms of extra shelving and rods that you might need to add to your newly organized closet. Get rid of any wire hangers, and put your clothes on good plastic hangers and/or skirt and pant hangers. Plastic hangers have several advantages. Since they are thicker than wire ones, your clothes are less likely to get crushed. Plastic hangers also have notches to hang straps of gowns and thin-strapped blouses so that they won't fall off, and, they stay cleaner than wire hangers, which are natural dust collectors. Finally, everyone has experienced, at one time or another, the frustration of tangled wire hangers. Plastic hangers put an end to that annoyance. *Tip:* Since plastic hangers do take up room, you can mount a rod a few inches from the closet shelf, where you can store the empty hangers so that they don't take up room amongst your clothes and so that you can grab an empty hanger without digging through your clothes.

Within the closet, group your clothing by category (see examples, below), then arrange each category by color. This makes selecting and coordinating outfits much quicker and easier. Also, as you rehang your clothes, remove plastic wrap from the cleaners. This

This closet was designed with the gentleman's specific needs in mind. Special features of the closet include acrylic pull-out pallets to store T-shirts, polo shirts, and tennis shorts. Casual wear is organized on the right, with business and dress clothes on the left. (Not shown: a special nook that holds ties, belts, and hats.) Acknowledgment: Design by Maxine Ordesky, Beverly Hills, California. Photography by Lois Ellen Frank.

plastic only makes the garment difficult to see and is dangerous for children and pets.

Clothes Categories

Pants	Tops, Vests
Skirts	Shirts, Blouses
Suits	Jackets
Athletic Clothes	Sweaters
Lingerie	Dresses
Dressy Clothes	Shoes
Hats	Belts, Ties

Once you have done this you will be able to see what your hanging needs are. You may want to install a double-rod system, which effectively doubles the available closet space by putting one rod up over another, measured so that blouses and shirts can be hung on the top rod, and pants or skirts can be hung on the rod below. While the top rod is a bit higher than a normal single rod system, it is reachable, and makes selecting and coordinating outfits a breeze and takes up a minimum of closet space. Also allow room to install a partition so that you can section off the closet and install a single rod that leaves enough room for longer items, such as dresses and robes.

Most people have more separates than long clothing, so often this rod space does not have to take up a great deal of the closet space.

Another rod possibility is a movable rod, similar to the type that dry cleaners use, which brings the clothes that you need into view at the flip of a switch. This is especially good for senior citizens who don't want to stretch, bend, and grope into the far reaches of a closet. It is also handy in the larger custom closet where there is a substantial inventory of clothing to deal with (huge walk-ins or rooms that have been turned into closets are good places for these systems).

If your closet has a hinged door, don't forget the portable rod that can be clipped onto a door to hold several hanging items. These are good for things you get to often, such as robes or jackets that you wear frequently, and can give you that much needed extra twelve inches of hanging rod space in your closet. A hook on the other side of the door can be a temporary resting place to hang things that you take off at the end of the day, or to hang the outfit you are planning to wear the next day.

Foldables

Clothes that are not generally hung in the closet include underwear, sleepwear, socks and stockings, T-shirts, sweatshirts and exercise togs, shorts, and sweaters. These clothes should be gone through as ruthlessly as you have gone through everything else. Get rid of everything that doesn't fit, is the wrong color, is stupid (like some of those T-shirts with ridiculous statements that you once thought were so profound), as well as anything that is raggedy or out of date.

That done, the foldables can be stored in a basket system in the closet (these are especially good for underwear and athletic wear), in a small dresser (in or out of the closet), or on shelves in the closet. Drawers, whether they are in a dresser or custom-built into a closet system, can be better organized by placing dividers and other organizers into the drawer. This can be as simple as putting shoe boxes into a drawer to separate socks and stockings, or having built-in drawers with custom dividers included inside the drawer (to fit your lingerie or jewelry) designed into your closet.

Some things stay neater longer if they are put on a shelf rather than a drawer. T-shirts and sweaters, for instance, seem to do better on a shelf where you can see at a glance what's there and pull out what you need. A drawer invites rummaging to get at what lies at the bottom. Once you've done some digging in a drawer, there is usually little or no motivation (or time) to put things back in order. Somehow a shelf is easier to keep neater, especially if you install dividers to keep the stacks from toppling into one another. You can get inexpensive wire or Lucite dividers that you can snap onto the shelf, or you can have modular units custom-built into you closet for this purpose.

Along with sweaters and t-shirts, men's folded shirts can be stored on a shelf, or, in a walk-in, custom pull-out pallets can provide an organized way to store the clothes and make them instantly accessible at the same time. You can also have custom drawer space built into your closet, which could eliminate the need for a dresser in the bedroom itself, and will put all of your clothing in one concen-

These shelf dividers can eliminate the problem of collapsing piles of clothing on the closet shelf. Acknowledgment: Lillian Vernon Catalogue.

These plastic sweater boxes come in a variety of sizes and can be used to store out-of-season sweaters, ski gear, gloves, scarves, or anything else that can benefit from an organized approach to storing things on closet or cabinet shelves. Acknowledgment: Organizers from Rubbermaid.

trated area—the closet. Other storage solutions for foldables include using stackable see-through plastic sweater and lingerie boxes as well as underbed storage drawers for storing out-of-season clothes, thus freeing up drawer or shelf space for the clothes that you are wearing now. Cedar chests, wicker trunks, and vinyl storage units and bags can also provide storage space for out-of-season clothes.

Accessories

Belts. Belt styles change right along with waist measurements, so get rid of the ones that don't fit or are out of style. The remaining belts can be organized by color and size (thin or wide) and hung on a tie rack or on a grid and hook system mounted on a closet wall or inside of the door. You can also have custom-built cubbies built so that they can be rolled

and stored in the compartments, or you can roll them in a basket system in your closet or dressing area.

Gloves. Gloves can be stored in plastic shoe boxes on a shelf, in a basket system, or in a divided drawer. Organize them by color and purpose (i.e., winter gloves grouped together, evening gloves in another grouping). You might even want to think about keeping the gloves in an area near the front door—perhaps in a small commode in the foyer or in

These moire drawer organizers can be used to organize lingerie, jewelry, or accessories in dresser drawers. Acknowledgment: Photograph courtesy of Hold Everything Catalogue.

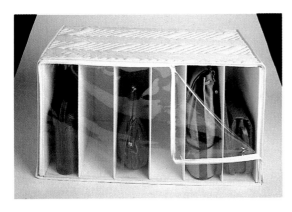

This handbag organizer keeps purses dust free and neatly visible on the closet shelf. Acknowledgment: Photograph courtesy of Hold Everything Catalogue.

a basket system in the coat closet where you can also store winter scarves and caps.

Handbags. Handbags can be stored efficiently on your closet shelf in a divided storage container (you can get these in quilted and vinyl or heavy cardboard materials). You can also hang a mug rack or a grid and hook system on the closet wall to suspend the handbags. If you're going custom, special cubbies for your handbags are the answer. Don't forget to measure your bags so that the cubbies can accommodate your small bags as well as your large, oversized tote bags.

Hats. Hat ownership depends on your fashion sense, personality, and the climate. The hats that you wear on a fairly regular basis can be organized and stored in several different ways:

- *Drawers:* If you've got any drawer space, knit hats and caps can be stored flat inside.
- *Boxes:* A plastic sweater box provides storage for out-of-season hats and caps, and can be put under the bed or on a closet shelf.
- *Baskets:* Winter caps and hats—especially the children's—can be stored in a basket by the door. Establishing the habit of dropping hats in the basket as soon as they're taken off can mean few missing hats and no more frantic searches for them on the way out of the door.
- *Pegs:* Hooks and pegs on the wall or on closet doors (and perhaps even on the back porch or door) also do a good job of holding hats. One simple peg system is an expanding wood mug rack that can be installed easily on the back of the door near the entry area.
- *Coat Trees:* These oldies but goodies are terrific in a corner of the entry and can hold coats *and* hats right where they are most needed, by the door.

- *Wig Forms:* Wig forms can be nailed to a closet shelf and dressy hats can be placed on the head, insuring that the hat keeps its shape and doesn't get squashed. These can be especially good for odd-sized hats that don't fit easily into a hat box. You might want to drape a piece of muslin or plastic over the hat so it doesn't get dusty on the wig form.
- *Hat Boxes:* Hat boxes are back and are available through catalogs and organizational retail shops. They can hold just about anything, but are especially good for holding *hats.*

Jewelry. Jewelry, like everything else, needs to be sorted with an eye to the possible elimination of some pieces. Jewelry that is tangled should be sorted out (work on it while you're watching TV), and jewelry that needs to be cleaned should be cleaned so you can wear it again.

Jewelry boxes are still good for storing jewelry, and today they come in all sizes, from small to a size that is practically a piece of furniture. If you go the box route, make sure you select one that is big enough to hold your jewelry comfortably without tangling. You can make your own jewelry center by turning a drawer into a jewelry "box." Do it yourself with drawer dividers, which are available in a variety of materials from plastic to fabric-covered divided trays. Or have the drawers custom-fitted with divided compartments lined in felt or velvet and sized specifically to fit your earrings, necklaces, bracelets, and so forth. Store silver jewelry in special storage pouches treated to keep the jewelry tarnish free; attach a gift tag to the bag with the piece of jewelry noted on it so that you don't have to look

through each bag to find what you want when you need it. And, of course, really valuable jewelry should be stored in a safe or safety deposit box. Custom closet designers are now incorporating hidden safes into their closet designs for this purpose. Other storage ideas for jewelry include:
- *Earrings:* Earrings can be hooked onto an earring holder (often made in clear Lucite with slots for holding pierced earrings). You can also place a piece of foam in a drawer, and stick post earrings into the foam. Keep the backs in a small separate box in the drawer.
- *Necklaces:* Necklaces can be kept in good order by hanging them on hooks or on a chain keeper (a chain keeper is generally made of clear plastic, holds several necklaces, and sits on top of a counter or dresser). You can also hang a mug rack in your closet or in the dressing area to hang your necklaces — tangle free and in clear view for easier selection when you dress.
- *Pins:* Pins can be kept in their own small jewelry box, or stuck into a pretty small satin pillow that you can keep inside a drawer or on your dressing table.
- *Rings:* Rings are easily lost, and usually have sentimental value, so giving them their own special resting place in a small ring box (these will hold several rings) or drawer can be a good idea. If you take off rings when you shower or wash dishes, have a hook or covered box next to the sink so that you automatically put the rings there when you take them off. You can also get a ring tree (usually made of porcelain) that holds rings, one on top of the other.

Scarves. Scarves can be stored in a drawer, basket, or plastic lingerie box on a shelf. If you do wear some scarves all of the time, you can keep these on hooks in the closet or on a mug

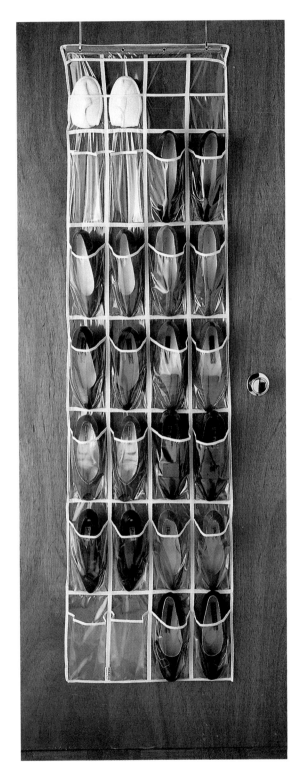

rack mounted on the inside of the closet drawer. Winter scarves can be stored near the door in the coat closet in a basket system or on hooks on the back of the door, or on the coat tree in the entry.

Shoes and Boots. Storage options for your shoes include:

- *Shoe Rack:* Shoe racks that hang over the inside of the closet door or sit on the closet floor can hold as many as twenty-four pairs of shoes. The metal racks are sturdy and can give you a good look at your choices for footwear at a glance.
- *Shoe Bags:* Hanging shoe bags serve the same purpose as the racks and can be hung on the inside or back of a door. There are also shoe bags now that can be hung inside the closet; because the bags are closed on the sides, the shoes don't touch the clothes on either side.
- *Shoe Boxes:* Plastic shoe boxes can hold shoes and can be stacked on the floor or on shelves. You can stack dressy shoes in boxes near your dressy clothes and casual shoes near your sporty attire with these boxes.
- *Shoe Cubbies:* Custom built shoe cubbies give you a special cubicle for each pair of shoes. To maximize space, store your shoes in the cubby with one shoe going in the space heel first, and the other shoe going into the space toe first.
- *Boot Trees:* Put boot trees inside your boots and they can be kept neatly either on the floor or on a shelf.
- *Boot Center:* You can establish a boot center

This over-the-door shoe bag organizer can hold up to fourteen pairs of shoes on the back of the closet or bedroom door. Acknowledgment: Lillian Vernon Catalogue.

during the times boots are frequently worn by staking out a corner inside the back door (or front door if you have an apartment). Put a large plastic dishpan in the corner so that galoshes can be immediately removed and put into the pan for drying. A kitty litter pan is good if there are lots of boot-wearing family members. You can also consider installing some low shelves near the entry if there are several pairs of boots at any given time. This way, the boots are where they should be at all times—near the door, ready to put on feet that are ready to walk out into the elements.

Socks and Stockings. Socks and stockings can be tough to keep neat and organized regardless of how you store them. Keep the jumble down to a minimum by tossing any stockings that have runs and getting rid of socks with no mate. The good socks and stockings can be stored in drawers which can be kept a bit neater with dividers. You can put two clear shoe boxes inside the drawer, for instance, with light-colored socks or stockings in one, and dark ones in the other. There are also some clear drawer dividers that you can buy that are bigger than cutlery or jewelry dividers and can be used to help keep the stocking or underwear drawer organized. Stocking bags are another storage option. These bags have pockets for stocking storage—one pair to a pocket—and can be hung directly in the closet or on a hook. You can put small children's socks in a bin on the floor of the closet next to their shoes, making it easier for them to dress and keep their things organized.

Be sure you periodically check your supply of socks and stockings so that you can pur-

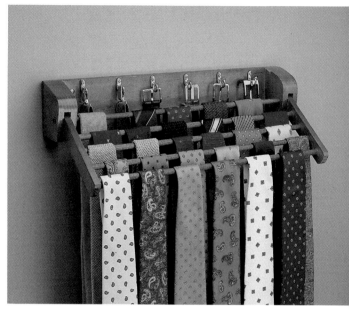

This wooden tie rack is easy to install and drops down into a flush position when not in use. Acknowledgment: Lillian Vernon Catalogue.

chase what you need *before* you run out. You should always have one pair of unopened stockings on hand for that very special occasion. Once you open that package, make a note to buy at least one new pair. Don't wait until you are completely out to run to the store (on the way to work or an event). Don't wait until your tennis socks are so stretched out that they are falling down around your ankles either. Stock up regularly and store your socks and stockings in an organized manner, and your feet and your life will be sweeter indeed.

Ties. Clothes organization and storage is not a problem faced only by women. For gentlemen, ties, as much as anything else, seem to proliferate unabated in the average closet. The easy-way-out gift for men, ties turn into

Tips from the Pros
Linda London, London Closet Company

Closet designer Linda London believes you can decorate your closet as nicely as you can your home and provide effective wardrobe storage at the same time. Her firm, London Closet Company, in New York City designs and installs customized closet systems and cabinetry in a variety of wood fabrications that includes mahogany, lacquer, laminate, and pickled woods. Whether she is designing a six-foot closet or an entire room that is being converted into a closet and dressing area, London's greatest challenge and satisfaction comes from creating her client's dream closet. She does this by combining functional design with special architectural and decorative touches. For that extra touch of elegance, you might want to incorporate some of London's special touches into your closet:

● **Color It Beautiful.** The closet, whether it's a walk-in master closet, or a smaller child's closet, can be painted in custom colors to either match or contrast with the walls of the room outside the closet. Cedar walls are especially nice for storage of winter clothing. The closet walls can also be covered in wallpaper or custom fabrics to coordinate with your design scheme in the bedroom. One idea is to mix tufted fabric on the wall or door with matching wallpaper for a truly special storage area.

● **Shelve It.** Shelving can be installed in a wide variety of fabrications, from exotic woods and finishes to glass. Bullnosing on the wood cabinetry and shelving, which is a technique for rounding off the edges of the cabinetry and shelving, can give the closet interior a more luxurious look. Or install moldings to give the closet a period look and add a finished architectural touch.

● **An Open and Shut Case.** The closet doors can be customized in any number of ways. For example, you can install French doors with glass panes as closet doors, giving the closet entrance the look of an armoire. If you wish, you can back the glass panes with shirred fabric to match other colors and fabrics in the room. (Touch-latch doors that open from the center to reveal the entire closet are a great improvement over sliding doors that only reveal a portion of the closet at one time.)

● **Completely Floored.** Don't forget the floors when you are decorating your closet. Custom ideas include carpeting, stenciling wood floors, or installing special tile. If your closet is a room, or even if you have designed and decorated it as a special (small) space in your bedroom, you won't necessarily have to match the flooring to that in the outer room. The closet stands on its own as a specially decorated and designed area.

● **It's What's Inside that Counts.** Drawers can be custom-cut to your specifications. For instance, you might want several smaller drawers as opposed to a few traditional deeper, bureau-type drawers. With the smaller drawers, you can keep your lingerie organized beautifully. You might want a "laundry" drawer just for your athletic togs, so that when you take them off, they don't soil anything else in the closet. The drawers are designed either with pulls or with grooves that eliminate the need for pulls, and provide a sleek, modern look. You can also have custom doors made to close over the drawers, giving you an armoire effect within your closet. And, you can have the drawer itself made from a wide selection of woods and other materials. You can even order drawers made of Plexiglas, allowing you a clear view of the contents at all times.

- **Divide and Conquer.** Drawer interiors can be customized in any number of fabrications. They can be divided with materials such as Plexiglas, special woods, or fabric-covered dividers. Velvet drawer interiors are perfect for jewelry, and moire taffeta provides a special setting for your lingerie.

- **Hardware Options.** Special hardware can provide a distinctive touch. Rods can be installed in chrome, Plexiglas, or brass, or they can be covered in shirred felt or other fabrics. Drawer pulls can be selected from porcelain, brass, chrome, colored plastic, wood, and mirrored materials. You can find them with special finishes or hand-painted designs as well. Tie racks, belt racks, and accessory hooks come in a wide range of styles and prices (a hook can cost from $2.50 to $100.00) to provide much-needed hanging accessible storage.

- **Lighten Up.** Lighting is a must for good viewing and selection of your clothing in the proper atmosphere. Rather than a bare bulb or spotlight which can be hard on your clothes (direct light tends to break down and fade fine fabrics), you might want to consider a chandelier for your walk-in. A small chandelier provides just the right amount of light, and when paired with a lovely rug on the closet floor, gives the space an elegant air.

- **Dressing Room for Success.** Large walk-ins or wardrobe rooms should have a design that includes a dressing area so that selecting your wardrobe and dressing can all be done in one private area. The creative possibilities for this concept are endless and can give you a quiet retreat for dressing beautifully for any occasion.

senseless clutter sooner or later, draped over wire hangers or hung haphazardly on hooks, nails, and tie racks. To sort out the tangle of ties, first get rid of the ties that you never wore and won't ever wear. A handful of ties is all the average man ever needs, and if somebody insists that dozens of ties are necessary to look good, simply reply that ties can only go around one neck, one at a time.

Put the wearable ties on a tie rack. These racks come in all sizes and shapes, with some of them even motorized so that at the push of a button the ties swing around into view, one at a time. If you don't want a fandangled tie rack, you can install a curtain rod on the back of the bedroom door and hang your ties there.

Even small children can benefit from simple storage systems. Acknowledgment: Pelly Industri AB Space Systems.

Chapter 9:
Children's Rooms

Children, whether they are six months or sixteen years old, claim ownership to an ever-changing inventory of belongings that beg for creative, functional storage. Depending on the child's age, the room could be overrun with diaper and other baby gear, toys, books, school papers and art projects, clothing and shoes of every size and description, games, half-finished science projects, sports equipment, magazines, and more. Eventually, particularly in the case of the smaller child, the clutter starts to creep into other areas of the house, requiring constant policing. Children often seem resistant to these "clean up your act" efforts, yet given half a chance and some storage space that fits their specific needs, many children will readily pick up after themselves, keeping their things organized and contained within one area—their rooms.

Before you plan new storage facilities for the kids, go through all of their things with them (this may be impossible with a teenager—more on that later). Get rid of toys that are broken or never used any more. All clothes that no longer fit (including baby clothes) should also go. Charities that serve families are always looking for serviceable children's things, and you can teach your child the value of charity and organization at the same time by letting him or her actively participate in this weeding out process.

If more than one child shares the room, it is important to allocate personal space for each child along with the shared space. Beds that have built-in storage can provide this individual space, as can desks that divide a room in half or are placed at the end of the bed, or under a loft bed. All storage space, be it closet space or toy storage space, should be divided as equally as possible. And whether or not your children share a room, it is important that you involve them in the space planning process—after all, they will be using the room, and they're more likely to keep it neat if they have a say in how it is arranged.

Cabinetry and Shelving

Before installing new shelving and storage cabinetry in the room, consider the current needs of the child as well as what those needs will be two years, four years, and six years from now. By installing adjustable fixtures, you can accommodate today's needs while allowing for future growth. If your child is at the age where s/he wants to display a model car or stuffed animal collection, provide some shelving for that purpose. Just make sure the collection is displayed on shelves that can later be used for books. For best results, install shelving and cabinetry at the child's eye level. If the storage is too high for them to reach, they will never put things away, and clutter will be a constant problem.

Hooks and pegs at the child's level are good for holding clothes, school bags, and large cotton or canvas bags for toys or school supplies (a simple mug rack on the back of the door is

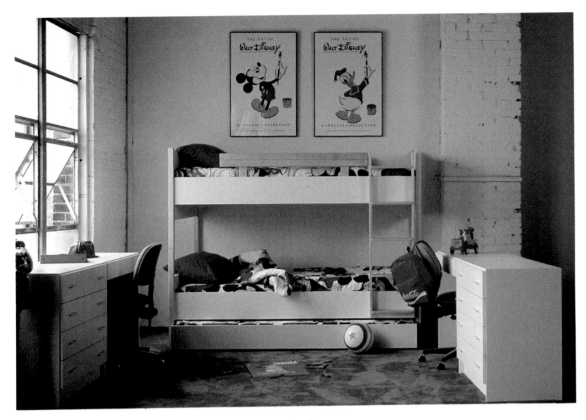

If more than one child shares a room, bunk beds can save precious space that can then be used for storage and study needs. Acknowledgment: Techline by Marshall Erdman & Associates, Madison, Wisconsin. Photo by Steven Rhyner.

great for this). Shelves can be installed with closed cabinet doors, or as open shelving. The open shelving is generally easier for small children to deal with, but you might want to put in shelving that can be adapted by adding door fronts in the later teen years. Games, books, and stuffed animals are easily stored on these shelves, and as the child gets older, records, cassettes, magazines, and collections can also be stored on the same shelves. For the younger child, a wide assortment of things—from puzzles to crayons—can be stored in bins (such as a dishpan or kitty litter pan) on the shelves, making putting things away simple enough, and giving the child a portable carryall to move the things back and forth from one area to another. Shelves and rods in the closet should also be installed to grow with the child.

Bunkbeds or beds with built-in bookcase headboards can go a long way toward helping organize and contain some of the everyday personal clutter. Underbed storage drawers or beds with built-in drawers can be useful for storing the child's belongings or for storing the linens that fit that bed.

Clothes and Shoes

One of the reasons children's drawers are always so messy is that every time they want something, they have to dig through the top layers of clothing to get to it (this problem is not unique to children—adults share the guilt). Open bins on shelves in the closet can work better than drawers, particularly for things such as underwear and socks. Or rolling basket systems can be used in the closet to hold everything from pajamas to cold weather hats and gloves. Shelves in the closet are good for T-shirts, sweaters, and shorts. You can label the shelves if you want so that the child learns to group like items together, and gradually, as the children get older, their folding skills will improve to match their already acquired organizing skills.

For very small tots, hanging up clothes on hooks in the closet is far simpler to deal with than hanging them on hangers (though you can install the rod at an adjustable height and the child can grow up to it). A large bin or underbed storage drawer can be the place for shoes. The shoes may get tossed in willy nilly, but at least they'll be in one place, and you'll reduce the number of times you have to find the missing shoe. Finally, kids are more likely to deposit dirty clothes if they don't have to go very far to do it so keep a hamper or a large canvas or cotton bag in the room for dirty clothes. The bag can hang by a cord from the closet or bedroom doorknob.

Games

Games usually come in boxes, which get

Baskets and rods positioned at lower levels can make it easier for children to keep their clothes in order. Acknowledgment: Techline by Marshall Erdman & Associates, Madison, Wisconsin. Photo by Steven Rhyner.

stacked until the pile resembles a construction site. As soon as one game is pulled out from the stack, the stack collapses. Or, the heavier boxes somehow move to the top by default, crushing all the boxes below. Obviously, games that are never played, or games that have permanently missing pieces (making them unplayable), should either be given away or tossed. Deniece Schofield, author of *Confessions of an Organized Housewife* and mother of five children, wrestled with this problem and finally came up with what is probably the best solution to the care and storage of games. Game boards and pieces are removed from the box, the boards are stacked on a shelf, and the pieces stored in a metal parts cabinet (these cabinets have lots of different-sized drawers). Deniece cuts the game directions from the lid of the box, photocopies them, and puts the copies in a looseleaf notebook in alphabetical order. Directions in pamphlet form are simply hole-punched and put into the binder. This method saves space, and helps cut down on lost parts, directions, and mangled boxes. The inevitable few games that have parts that are too big for the cabinet can be stored in plastic shoe boxes and put on the shelf next to the boards.

Hobby Paraphernalia

Hobby paraphernalia, whether it's model airplane parts or tempera paints, needs to be stored in a concentrated area in the room (as opposed to all over the room). A cabinet that holds bins with the various supplies is one answer, and if it is only about two shelves high, the child can use the top of the cabinet as a work table. Another option is a table with a rolling basket system either next to, or under,

the table—again, this provides work space and keeps all the necessary equipment close at hand. As the child gets older, or if the collection of parts and supplies becomes excessive, you can always go to shelving on the wall over the worktable. Again, bins are the simplest way to group and store supplies, particularly the smaller items. Besides dishpan-type bins, clear plastic shoe boxes are effective containers that stack nicely and provide a clear view of the contents.

School Papers and Art Projects

The minute a child starts school, you can expect the volume of paper in the house to at least quadruple. For parents who have never known where to put the children's school papers and art projects that are so proudly handed over each day, the answer is in a rolling basket system. Simply turn it into a filing cart by hanging Pendaflex files on rails (you can purchase these with the cart). Label the files Awards, Arithmetic, Spelling, Writing, and so on. Inside each Pendaflex file, place a manila file folder with the same label. Then, after you have fussed glowingly over your child's accomplishments of the day, walk over to the rolling basket file and help your child file the papers. The oversized art projects can be stored in the baskets below, with smaller pieces being temporarily displayed on a bulletin board in the child's room. This system teaches and creates organization and storage at the same time; just be sure to have a basket system for each child to eliminate all of the problems that go along with sharing.

At the end of the school year, remove the manila file folders, sort through them with the child, and save the best. Put your selections in a transfile box, mark it with your child's age and the year, and store it in an inactive area, such as the back of the closet.

Be careful not to get carried away by keeping every scrap of paper the child brings home; if you do, you'll need to rent a warehouse to store it all. Rather, a cabinet in the garage or basement, or a shelf or two in a spare closet should be the designated spot; when the storage area gets full, it's time to go back and be a bit more cold-blooded about throwing some papers away. This cart should take your child through high school, serving as a school records and supply center that can be rolled to the homework area as needed. When the child finally leaves the nest, you can use the cart yourself for clothes, projects, or hobby or stationery supplies.

Sports Equipment

Sports equipment, if it is not stored in another area of the house (such as the basement or a spare closet turned "sports center"), can be effectively stored in a child's room by assigning an area for just that purpose. A small section of the closet that allows standing room for taller items and shelves with bins can hold everything from bats and hockey sticks to balls and pucks. Sports uniforms can go on hooks next to this center, and balls can be tossed into an all-purpose trash can in the same area (the size of the can should match the number and size of balls that need to be stored). Other hooks in the area can be used to keep hats, mitts, or anything else that can be hung stored neatly and effectively. Bins on shelves are good for keeping smaller items such as swim goggles or knee pads together. If there is no room for this "sports center" in the closet, you can turn a corner into sports storage with shelves, bins, hooks, and the can for balls. A rolling basket system can take the place of shelves and keep the gear organized by category or by child if more than one little person stores their equipment in this area.

Stuffed Animals

Stuffed animals are usually an adult problem. Generally children outgrow their stuffed animals and, except for one or two favorites, don't even notice when the collection is given away. It's the parents who have a hard time giving up these critters. If your kid is sixteen, and you're still hanging on to that tattered bear and cute rabbit, it's time to let go.

If, on the other hand, your child is still at an age where animals are important, you can store the excess (after all, the child probably only really likes a select few) in a wicker trunk, wicker basket, or window seat. Shelves on the wall can provide storage and display space, and for the stuffed animals that have definitely been shunted aside by the little owner, you can install a shelf along the molding at the top of the wall where you can display the animals, slowly moving them toward the door and out of the room to charity.

Toys

Keeping up with toy clutter can be the biggest organizational and storage problem of all. The kids scatter toys from one end of the house to the other, and when it comes time to pick them all up and put them away, the children mysteriously disappear. The traditional toy box is no longer the answer, since invariably, the toys get piled into the box, and when the child wants something from the box, nearly

Tips from the Pros
Deniece Schofield, Author

Mother of five children, and daughter of a very organized mother, Deniece Schofield was an organizational late bloomer. As a child, she was so disorganized that her mother thought she was hopeless. Coming home to a bed piled high with belongings that her mother had put there for Deniece to put away posed no problem; Deniece simply wrapped the mess up in the bedspread and moved the pile to the floor. As an adult with three children she "hit bottom" when keeping up with her daily obligations became so overwhelming that she knew she had no choice but to make some changes. She decided she had to get *organized*. Over the following years she developed a system of organization that was so simple and effective that she wrote several books on the subject, including *Confessions of an Organized Housewife* and *Confessions of an Organized Family*. She has a wealth of information on keeping children organized, and she has some particularly helpful advice for people who are expecting their very own bundle of joy:

• **Don't Buy Out the Store.** Just because the baby is coming doesn't mean you have to buy every baby gadget, doodad, or piece of furniture that you see in the stores. Remember that these things have to be stored somewhere, and if you have limited space, this could be a problem, so be selective with your purchases.

• **Shop for Dual Function.** The biggest mistake people make is to buy something that only performs one function. For example, a baby bathtub is usually made out of molded plas-

tic, impossible to fold up for storage, and usually only good for only about three months, when the baby outgrows the tub. A more creative idea is to use a laundry basket. Simply place baby in the basket and put the basket in the bathtub and fill the tub with just enough water to do the job. The basket does double duty as a laundry basket and won't require additional storage space. Another example is the purchase of a playpen, which Schofield advises against since they are expensive, take up room, and may, according to some experts, stifle creativity in children. Instead, Schofield uses a tension gate stretched across a door to make an entire room into a playpen, so the baby can play in his/her room while you iron or do paperwork just outside the gate. The child has more room, and so do you since you never have to worry about storing the playpen.

• **Store Diapers in a Dishpan.** Take diapers out of the box and stand them upright in the dishpan (which come in a variety of colors to match your decor); keep a box of sandwich baggies nearby so that the diaper duty is simply organized. The dishpan is easy to move, and can be quickly stowed in a cabinet if you want to spruce the room up for company.

• **Store Baby Toiletries in a Child's Hanging Shoebag.** You can hang the bag near the crib or changing table, or keep it in the bathroom so that everything is handy, and neatly stored as well.

• **Store Bathtub Toys in a Mesh Bag.** The bag can be hung over the shower head so that the toys drip dry, and are easy to get to when you need them but not really in the way when you don't.

• **Buy a Crib that Stores Easily.** When you buy your first crib, make sure that it can fold down when the child outgrows it (you'll need it for the next baby). Safety considerations make cribs a good investment, but don't forget future storage considerations when you make the purchase.

- **Use Towel Racks.** A towel rack installed above the dressing table or at the end of the crib can be a perfect way to keep towels at hand without taking up table top space. Likewise, a towel bar installed on the back of a high chair can be the answer to storing a bib and washcloth for cleaning up baby's food spills and face.

- **Use Drawer Dividers.** To keep baby clothes in drawers in some kind of order, try using child-sized shoe boxes or large plastic food storage containers as separators. It helps reduce the jumble, and therefore the search for the sleeper or tiny socks when you need them.

Baby supplies can be kept close at hand near the crib or changing table with this wall-mounted wire storage rack. Acknowledgment: Modulus, Chicago, Illinois.

everything gets dragged out of the box in search of the desired toy, which is usually at the bottom. To avoid this cycle of clutter, think in terms of storing toys by category; that way transferring them from one area to another is easy. Books, dolls, blocks, soldiers, crayons, etc., can be grouped separately and stored in plastic or rubber bins. Kitty litter pans, dishpans, baskets, and rolling toy cages can all be used to hold specific groups of items on shelves, in cabinets, or under the bed.

To help children keep the categories straight and teach them how to put things away, try taping a picture of, say, an animal (for stuffed animals) to the front of the bin or cage. For older children, use a flashcard with the category printed on it. Also, older children can store books on bookshelves, but for younger children, a simpler system is to stand the books upright in a bin. The children can then flip through the books and see the covers.

To facilitate end-of-the-day toy clutter cleanup, have the children put all of the toys into a rolling toy cage or laundry basket so they can pull it back to their room where they can sort everything into the proper bin. The child can throw all of the toys into the basket, take it to his or her room, and distribute the toys in the bin. If the child regularly plays in, say, the den, you might want to set up a small cabinet there for the most frequently used toys. Stick to the bin/category system wherever the toys are stored, and keeping the toys stored will be simpler for you and your children.

Teenagers' Rooms

If you've got teenagers, chances are you know the real meaning of the word *chaos*. If they had trouble putting things away when they were little, now they are probably ready to enter the twilight zone of the totally, hopelessly disorganized. Add to this their general attitude—not always the greatest—and you can have a real problem on your hands. You could always shut the door to their rooms and forget about it, but we all know full well that if they don't get a handle on the organization/storage problem now, they'll grow up to be slobs, and the parent will get the blame (that's you).

Approaching the storage problem in this room can be tricky. Attitude is everything: It is imperative that you remain calm. Let your teenager know that some changes will be made. The teen may try to get hysterical, but ignore that tactic; it is meant to wear you down. Explain that he or she will be participating on every level, with many of the decisions falling to him or her. Whatever changes you make, never refer to it as "work"; rather, solving the storage problem will be done as a "project." This project should be perceived as a challenge and a goal that will bring its own rewards once achieved. Remind your teen that by completing this project, everybody will be better off. You won't have to nag about the out-of-the-open mess, and the teen won't have to keep thinking up ways of getting out of cleaning up the mess.

Assessing the teen's needs is crucial. At the same time, cast an eye to the future use of the room. Whatever a teen needs today is probably not what he or she will need eight months from now. A thirteen-year-old boy may collect model cars, but by the time he's fifteen, he's looking to own a car and couldn't care less about his car collection. An adolescent girl grows into beauty paraphernalia at an astounding rate; starting with a tube of lipstick she quickly comes to "need" an entire vanity full of cosmetics, hair potions, and accessories, all of which requires everchanging or expanding storage in her room.

Cabinetry and/or shelving can be installed on spare walls with very little thought to height, maximizing the amount of storage space available. Freestanding shelving can be anything from wicker to heavy-duty modular, and can be selected based on you and your teen's preferences. These units can accommodate books, trophies, collections, memorabilia, stereo and TV equipment, and records and tapes (in tape caddies or racks) by the dozens. Attractive baskets holding grouped items can be stored on the shelves to contain such things as hair accessories, correspondence, and change.

Finally, if your children plan to leave the nest for college or freedom, don't lose sight of the possible uses for the room after their departure. By making simple adjustable changes now, you can turn the room into a functional space for now and well into the future.

Clothing and Shoes

If the closet needs an overhaul, now may be the time to invest in a completely new system, giving the teen lots of storage space that can serve you just as well when he or she leaves home. A double-rod system with shelves and shoe cubbies or over-the-door shoe racks are useful, regardless of who is using the closet. Sweaters and T-shirts will

Plan your child's room with the future in mind. Here, storage and study areas can be easily adapted to take a child through her teen years comfortably. Acknowledgment: Techline by Marshall Erdman & Associates, Madison, Wisconsin. Photo by Steven Rhyner.

be kept a bit neater if they are folded and put on shelves rather than stuffed into drawers. Hooks for everyday jackets, caps, hats, belts, and handbags (a mug rack will do) are very serviceable and can be used strictly for storage or to display things (such as a hat collection). Rolling baskets can be used for clothing in the closet (these are particularly good for underwear, stockings, and exercise clothing), and a clothes hamper will cut down on the piles of dirty clothes otherwise found all over the room.

Papers

A rolling basket system can serve as a rolling file and supply station for school work or ongoing paper projects. A good desk will also help contain and control the paper clutter and provide a sensible workspace for your teen at the same time (plus you'll have a useful piece of furniture yourself later). Make sure the desk has ample drawer space for basic supplies, and a reasonably roomy desktop for work space. A table can serve as a desk in a pinch, but it invites rampant clutter and confusion, so your best bet is to invest in a serviceable desk.

You may also want to invest in a small two-drawer filing cabinet for paper and file storage. This can be placed immediately to the right of the desk, tucked into the closet, or used as a nightstand next to the bed. If there's a computer, a computer stand will hold the equipment in an organized manner (rolling baskets make good supply stations to have near these stations).

Extra Teen Gear

If your teen is a tinkerer, with lots of wires and hardware all over the place, a pegboard and hook system and a metal parts cabinet can do the storage trick, as can tackle and tool boxes. For larger items, such as craft supplies, plastic shoe or sweater boxes can keep things organized and stacked neatly when stored. The pegboard and hook system can also be used for jewelry, hair ribbons, or handbags. Teens with lots of nail polishes and cosmetics can organize drawers and shelves with divider inserts, or they can use easy-to-carry plastic divided trays and caddies made expressly for storing such items.

Of course, all the storage space in the world won't guarantee that your children will keep their things stored neatly and sensibly in their rooms. But providing the space at least puts the excuses to rest. Now they should have room for everything, and it's up to you to figure out how to get them to put everything away in that room. Good luck.

A closet wall unit in the spare room can accommodate decorative and entertainment items as well as books and visitors' clothes. Acknowledgment: Techline by Marshall Erdman & Associates, Madison, Wisconsin. Photo by Steven Rhyner.

Chapter 10:
Spare Room

Spare room describes a part of the house where there is rarely any *spare room*. What starts out as an extra room often ends up as a dumping ground for all manner of things — from household financial records to craft supplies. Hidden beneath the clutter is a guest bed that is rarely used because the rest of the room is such a mess that inviting overnight guests in becomes unthinkable.

Spare rooms today are used as guest rooms, home offices (for more on home office use, see Chapter 11), den/libraries, and hobby rooms. They are also used frequently for storage of a multitude of things from around the house that don't seem to fit anywhere else. The first step in organizing the storage and closet space in this room is to focus on the use of the room. This is particularly important if the room serves more than one purpose, i.e., if it is used as a serving center and as an exercise room. For multipurpose rooms, a good rule of thumb is to section off space for each function. You don't want to fall over barbells to get to the thread, and you shouldn't have to rummage through fabric bolts to find your leg weights. Whether the room serves one purpose or several purposes, making it functional as well as pleasant will turn the room into an invitation to work, rest, or pursue your favorite hobby.

Cabinetry and Shelving

Since the spare room is often used as a multi-purpose room or to store a wide variety of things, it can be the room that benefits the most from customized shelving and cabinetry. If you are using and storing arts and crafts supplies, sewing supplies, or other specialized equipment, you can usually triple your space with custom nooks, shelves, and cabinets built especially to accommodate odd-shaped hobby gear. Take stock of all of your supplies (don't forget to count all of that fabric or those tubes of paint shoved into drawers and the back of the closet), so you can design storage space that really will hold everything and make it all easy to get to at the same time.

Boxes

Books can accumulate with frightening speed. Bookaholics fill spare rooms with boxes and bags of books long after all available bookcases have been filled past capacity. For these people, floor-to-ceiling bookcases are a must for the spare room. Beyond that, however, I recommend sharing the joy and pleasure that books can bring by passing them along. Keep a selection of those most special tomes, and when the bookcase gets full, weed out a stack to pass on. This simple technique gives you immediate storage space for your books (the bookshelves), at absolutely no cost to you.

Art and Art Supplies

If you or a member of your family is a budding artist, the spare room can become a studio easily enough, though exactly how to store all of the relevant art supplies in the room requires a bit more thought. Custom cabinetry may be the answer, and art supply stores can provide additional storage with their elaborate boxes, cabinets, and taborets, designed to provide special spaces for storing paints, brushes, and artwork. If your budget can't accommodate such solutions, look for creative alternatives. You can adapt a ceramic vase, coffee can, or large oatmeal box to hold brushes, or you can use an inexpensive tackle or tool box to corral some of your colorful artistic tools. These supply holders can be stored on a shelf built near your work area or in a closet. A narrow shelf will do the trick and take up a minimum of space.

Rolling basket systems can also become portable art centers for holding jars of paint, brushes, and art paper supplies. If you have art that can be rolled up, store it in large, clean, circular trash cans, or in architect's bins (these bins are expensive, but look terrific and are on wheels for easy movability). To store flat canvases, you might want to build a simple cabinet or adapt one you already have by adding plywood partitions to make slots to slide the canvases into for storage. Or, you can turn a small bookcase on end to convert it from a horizontal storage unit for books to a vertical storage unit for larger-sized art projects.

Craft Supplies

Craft supplies also generate hard-to-store clutter that can quickly turn into unmanageable piles. This is particularly true when there is more than one type of craft stored in a room (i.e., model train parts and knitting gear). Whether it's one craft or several, however, once the clutter takes over, the prospect of working on the craft seems to lose its magic,

with unfinished projects sitting forlornly in corners, boxes, bags, and drawers. Working on too many craft projects at once is asking for trouble, so the first step is to reduce the amount of supplies on hand along with some of the unfinished projects. Eliminate all but the most necessary or fun craft-related items. If you've got railroad accessories that don't go with anything, or odd skeins of fuchsia yarn that you'll never use, get rid of them so you only have to worry about storing the more important craft materials.

Once that's done, allocate a special area for each craft with a cabinet or chest for storage, along with, for example, shelves over a desk or worktable. Your worktable can be a simple folding card table, a drafting table, a kitchen table, or a table made from a hollow core door laid across two sawhorses or two two-drawer filing cabinets (the filing cabinets hold supplies). You can also create a worktable from a combination of basket systems topped by a formica or butcher block top; the baskets hold and separate supplies and keep them visible and instantly accessible. Rolling baskets can also be used to hold additional supplies or unfinished projects. When you're ready to work, simply pull the rolling basket over to your work area. You can store very small items in metal parts cabinets or tool or tackle boxes (check your local hardware or sporting goods store for these). Oatmeal cartons or coffee cans are still a good old-fashioned standby for holding things such as knitting needles and special brushes, and you can use a supply caddy (usually used to hold cleaning supplies) to store items that can be easily carried from storage to the work area. Other great inexpensive containers for various supplies are plastic and rubber bins, dishpans, and cat litter pans—all of which can be stored on shelves, in drawers, or under the bed. Don't forget the potential for window seat storage, which can hold supplies and provide a place to sit and work at the same time.

Exercise Equipment

If ever there was a case for "use it or lose it," this is it. If you decide to use it, there's no point in spending lots of time and money trying to store it—be it barbells or an exercise bike—because the fact is, if you have to fuss, you won't get the stuff out and put it back again. Although you can store some of the equipment in bins or cabinets, you'll probably be better off in the long run if you simply allocate an area of the room (maybe the entire room) to serve as your workout center. Keep all of your equipment in that area so that you can just walk over to your "gym" and start exercising without worrying about pulling out and putting back your gear. Don't think of the equipment as an eyesore, think of it as a daily personal achievement. I guarantee that people who see it won't stop to think about how it clutters up the room. They'll be too busy thinking that they really should be exercising themselves.

Guest Rooms

Most spare rooms start out as a potential guest room before they turn into store rooms. To make use of your spare room as both a guest room and a room for storage (for things such as out-of-season clothes, hobby supplies, etc.), think carefully about the furniture that goes into the room. A chest or small cabinet

can double as a nightstand, and beds with built-in storage drawers can give your guests a place to slumber and you a place to store blankets and sheets. Wall units are always good and can store your book overflow, a small radio and television, and decorative square baskets, small chests, or boxes with tops that can provide storage for everything from sewing notions to past tax records. A cedar chest or window seat can give you additional attractive storage space without compromising the guest room features, and you can have a system designed for the guest closet that will maximize the space so that you can use at least half of the closet for storage, yet still provide some empty space for the guest's things. Basket systems or small chests inside the closet can hold everything from extra linens to memorabilia, behind closed doors. Hooks on the back of the guest room door add a nice touch for the guest, and give you a spot to hang things temporarily when needed.

If you must use the guest room for other activities, you may want to try camouflaging the storage or activity-related things. For instance, you can turn the closet into a sewing or hobby center. Add a drop-down table mounted on the closet door or wall next to the closet, and you have a "portable" activity and storage center that can be closed inconspicuously when guests are in residence.

If you enjoy having guests, you should make your guest room pleasant and easily available. Remember when you walk into the room to store something that the room's primary purpose is to serve as a guest room. If you can't store something discreetly in the room (stacking in the corner and piling on the bed is not allowed here), then store it somewhere else. Nothing is more aggravating than trying to turn a spare room that has become a store room into a guest room on short notice.

Sewing Supplies

It's all too easy for sewing supplies to take up as much as a room's worth of space, hence, "sewing rooms." But unless you are really serious about sewing, there's no reason to keep dozens of zippers, ribbons, trims, buttons, threads, patterns, and fabric scraps of every description and size. Menders need keep only the basics: threads, seam ripper, needles, buttons, and a few snaps. These should be stored with a pair of scissors in a compartmentalized sewing basket which keeps everything neatly organized and can be stashed on any handy cabinet or closet shelf. Procrastinating menders, beware. If you've got piles of clothes accumulating in bags and boxes that you're going to get to "someday," it's time to take action. Start fresh by taking everything to your local tailor or seamstress. Then, as new mending projects pop up, take ten or fifteen minutes in the evening to sew on that one button or fix that hem before the mending piles up again.

Serious sewers present another side of the story. They are convinced that they need a complete inventory of everything from bobbins to rick-rack to interfacing. If you find yourself consistently going past the same piece of fabric or never looking at a pattern after the first time you use it, remember that you'll be more productive with your current sewing projects if you don't have to constantly dig past stuff you don't intend to use. Unload the excess by giving it to friends, relatives, or charity.

The sewing notions that you keep because you know you'll use them can be stored in plastic shoe boxes with labels. These boxes stack neatly on the shelves or on the floor and you can see at a glance how many blue zippers, for example, are in the zipper box. Wicker and small plastic baskets can also hold notions as can small parts cabinets (good, for instance, for buttons). A cup rack mounted on the wall can hold scissors and such, and a pegboard and hook system can also handle your storage needs for notions, particularly large spools of thread.

Patterns never seem to fit back into the envelope once they've been unfolded, but there is a simple way to store them so that they can be used again. Put each pattern into a nine-by-twelve-inch manila envelope, then cut the pattern envelope open, and attach it to the front of the manila envelope. That way your patterns will stay organized and easy to retrieve when you need them. You can store the nine-by-twelve-inch envelopes upright in a bin or kitty litter pan which can be stored on a closet shelf or, if your guest bed is high enough, under the bed.

The average sewing room finds fabric in large folded pieces, on bolts, or in scrap piles. Bolts of fabric are often kept for that major project you're going to get to someday. Today is as good a someday as any other, so get to it. Bolts that you're certain you're going to use should be covered in plastic and stored under the bed, or upright in a round small plastic trash can. Architect's bins are also good storage holders for these unwieldy rolls.

You can make your own sewing work and storage center in your spare room by placing a top over two basket systems. The baskets hold more than a conventional desk or sewing machine cabinet and can keep scraps and larger pieces of fabric neatly organized near the machine. Acknowledgment: Norscan® Scanimport America, Staten Island, New York.

Large pieces of fabrics can be folded around a piece of cardboard and stored in an underbed storage drawer or on a shelf, and smaller pieces can be put in plastic sweater bags or boxes and stored on a shelf, under the bed, or in a rolling basket system.

As for the scraps, if you think about it, it's hard to justify allocating spare space for hundreds of bits and pieces. Scraps should be used, turned into rags, given to a quilting society, or tossed. The scraps that you just can't part with can be stored, folded in large plastic Ziploc storage bags. This helps keep them organized and makes it easier to sort through them. The bags can be stored in a covered basket or plastic sweater box (if you have more than one box full, they can be stacked easily on the closet shelf or floor). If Ziploc bags seem like too much trouble, keep one large bag or basket of scraps, but when it gets full, throw some away before you add any more to the pile.

Wire basket systems placed in the closet, under a worktable, or against a wall can keep your fabrics neatly sorted by color and weight, and make each piece a cinch to get to (no more digging through a huge pile on the closet shelf; simply pull out the basket with the fabric you want). Fabric can also be hung over hangers and kept in the closet. Finally, to make your fabric supply really functional, you can buy some string pricing tabs (check your stationery store or a store that supplies retailers) to hang on the fabric hangers. Note the

yardage and the date on the tag and loop it on the hanger; attach the tags to folded pieces with a pin. Whenever you use some of the fabric, make an additional note on the tag, or make out a new one, and you'll always know how much yardage you have to work with so that you can accurately project any pattern's fabric possibilities.

Your spare room, properly organized and arranged, may be your guest room, den, library, office, sewing or crafts center, or it may serve so many functions that it becomes your project room. However you use this all-important space, a well-thought-out assessment of your storage needs—both active and inactive—along with some creative organizational ideas can turn this room into one of the most important rooms in the house.

A spare room can be converted to a guest room simply by pulling out a bed that is otherwise "stored" in the wall unit. Acknowledgment: Techline by Marshall Erdman & Associates, Madison, Wisconsin.

Tips from the Pros
Kathleen Poer, Spacial Designs

Founding member and officer of the San Francisco Chapter of the National Association of Professional Organizers, Kathleen Poer first got into the organizing business over ten years ago with her training firm, The Well Organized Woman. This business gradually evolved into the current business that Poer owns with her husband, Bob, Spacial Design. Spacial Design specializes in providing creative solutions to storage problems; they look for ways to do things differently so that people can find extra space in their homes. The "spare" room is often an area with tremendous possibility. To assess your spare room's storage potential, Poer recommends the following:

• **Take an Inventory.** Make a full assessment of your needs by making a list of everything you would like to do in the room.

• **Make a Plan.** Group activities together so that you can plan the space by creating "centers" for those activities. For example, if you want the room to accommodate an area for paperwork or study, as well as for a hobby, list the things that go with each activity, so you will know how much storage and active space you will need for each.

• **What Are Your Priorities?** Prioritize your space according to how it's used. Plan to have the most important items in the most accessible areas; you'll want thread near the sewing machine, for instance, but large bolts of fabric can be stored a few steps away in the closet.

• **Consider Traffic Patterns.** Keep traffic in mind as you plan; you don't want to have to go through a busy area to get to your area, and you don't want a lot of traffic going through "quiet" areas.

• **Yours, Mine, and Ours.** Allocate space appropriately. If the space is shared, make sure that the allocation is fair. Once that allocation has been made, make sure everyone agrees to work within his or her own space.

• **Look for Creative Solutions.** Don't get locked into tradition. For example, you can turn a linen closet into a small sewing center and store the linens in the rooms where they are actually used. Use your imagination and be creative with your space. Creative Idea: A filing cabinet or bookcase can be used as a room divider, and if you put cork on the back of it, you can use the back as a portable "wall" for temporary storage of important reminders and phone numbers by your desk.

• **Reevaluate Use of Furniture.** Check to see what you already have that could be put to better use for space-saving storage. Baskets, organizing containers, bins, racks, chests, trunks, and functional furniture can all be put to use effectively for storage.

• **Seek Professional Help.** If you are so pressed for extra space that you are convinced that you'll have to move to have enough storage, you might want to consider custom-designed systems. Although you can increase available storage space by installing a freestanding system yourself, these will save you only inches or feet, while a custom design might actually *double* that available storage space.

You can turn a corner into an office with some
careful planning and clever storage and furniture combinations. Acknowledgment: Techline
by Marshall Erdman & Associates, Madison,
Wisconsin. Photo by Steven Rhyner.

Chapter 11:
Home Office

These days, almost every home needs some kind of "office." Even if all you do is pay bills and keep track of the children's scheduling obligations, the paper that's generated should be readily accessible when needed. From that starting point, the home office possibilities can expand to the storage requirements of people who have a business that they run from their homes. Part-time writers, computer geniuses, and paper clippers (people who compulsively clip articles because they might need that information someday), add yet another dimension to the potential need for office-type storage in the home. Finally, even if you don't think you need an office in the home, the question of the mail invariably rears its ugly paper head. What do you do with it when it comes in? After it's read, paid, or considered, where exactly do you put it? If you're dealing with paper in a minimal, part-time way, or are a full-blown business with paper coming out of your ears, your first step is to implement proper storage.

Cabinetry and Shelving

Wherever your office is, whether it's a corner in the kitchen or an entire room in the house, shelving can be a good place to start to provide extra storage. A wall unit can have a leaf that extends to provide a small table for paying bills and writing letters. Or you can build a wall unit around a freestanding desk. The unit can include closed cabinetry at the bottom to hold office supplies and stationery. The top portion of the unit can accommodate reference books, special mementos, and binders with chronological papers in them (such as board minutes if you are a member of a Board of Directors). Storing papers in binders frees up other file storage space, and if you don't need the papers often, you can put them on the higher shelves. You can buy freestanding units to hold computer equipment, but if you are really short on space, you can save inches by having a unit custom-built (since the freestanding units are often bigger than is actually necessary). If you are thinking of turning a spare room into an office or study space for two people, you can use a wall unit to divide the room into two equal spaces as well as to supply much needed storage space. Large closets can be turned into a small office center by fitting them with custom shelving around a desk or around a custom-built desk area. Long wall closets can be very good for this, providing ample room for computer equipment, typing materials, and storage for supplies. If you don't like the idea of such a confined space, you can turn your closet into a storage center that can be converted to hold all of your office files and supplies. Simply remove the rod and line the interior with shelving. You can also put a small chest of drawers, cabinet, or rolling basket system in the closet to store smaller things like pens, paper clips, and the like. Or you could use a basket system to store supplies, then roll it over to your work area whenever you need to. If you have limited wall or closet space, even two small shelves mounted over your desk area can be a lifesaver—to store a small supply of envelopes, paper, and other supplies that you use regularly.

Functional Furniture

The first piece of furniture people start thinking about in the home office is the desk, but too often they treat it as an aesthetic rather than a pragmatic decision. Be flexible about the design of the desk as it relates to your overall decor scheme. For example, if you have a lot of paperwork and your decor is fussy French, you will have a hard time finding a fussy French desk that will look good and give you adequate storage and work space. A good desk should have at least some drawer space for storing pens, pencils, clips, and other miscellaneous small supplies. Ideally, your desk will also have at least one drawer that will accommodate files. This drawer can then be used either for stationery supplies, household files (if you only have a few), or "active" files—things that you are currently working on. You can buy a desk to suit this idea or you can make your own by, say, putting a small desk with only small drawers (for the pens, etc.), next to a rolling file bin.

This wall unit can serve as a portable work space and requires absolutely no screws, nails, or fixtures for installation. Acknowledgment: The Tomorrow Group, Inc.

Other creative ways to give you a desk include stretching a piece of butcher block or a hollow-core door across two small two-drawer filing cabinets. You can compensate for lack of drawer space by installing a small shelf over the unit where you can put attractive bins to hold some of the smaller supplies. You can also purchase, from the stationery store, desktop organizers that have slots and cubbyholes for envelopes, paper, and such. Another variation of this idea is to create a desk out of a laminated or butcher-block top and wire basket system. The basket system serves as drawers for your supplies, and if, for example, this is used in your teenager's room for a desk, you can always dismantle it in the future and use the baskets in other areas of the house for other types of storage.

Credenzas or buffets will also provide good storage for office supplies. Since they're an attractive piece of furniture with shelves and drawers for storage, you can put them in just about any room without giving it an "office" effect. Metal cabinets, of course, also serve as office supply centers, and they could be put in a closet, hall, or perhaps in an enclosed porch. Two-shelf metal cabinets need not be too jarring to the senses; simply give them a coat of paint and put some plants or photos on top to dress 'em up a bit.

Furniture to hold typewriters, computers, or other office equipment is also available or can be created from custom shelving or furniture you have on hand. For typewriters, you might want to buy a desk that includes a typewriter return. Some desks (particularly older ones) have these fixed returns, while many newer desks have a rolling unit that slides partially under the desk or pulls out to provide more space next to the typewriter as needed. Or you could always resort to the traditional portable metal typewriter stand which can be stored in a closet or corner and rolled out when needed. Computer equipment can be housed in a computer center, or you can store the keyboard on your desktop, and buy a small add-on shelf that sits atop the desk to hold the monitor. Printers can then be stored next to the keyboard area. If your desktop doesn't have enough space, any small table (such as an end table) will probably do the job.

Provide long-term storage for papers in good filing cabinets. By "good," I mean cabinets that have drawers featuring full suspension systems. Bargain-rate filing cabinets often do not have this feature, making it difficult to get to papers at the back of the drawer (since the drawer does not pull out to its full extension when you open it) and providing

This compact, convenient, and mobile computer cart can hold your complete computer system in less than four square feet. Acknowledgment: O'Sullivan Industries.

less storage space overall than most full-suspension cabinets.

Depending on how many papers you have, you may want two-, three-, or four-drawer cabinets. Two-drawer cabinets have special value in the home since they can be placed immediately next to the desk area so that getting papers in and out of the file is effortless. It is also easy to store filing cabinets in nearly any closet. Or a rolling wire basket system can be converted so that the top holds files (about one small file cabinet drawer's worth), and you can store office supplies underneath. This basket system can also be stored in a closet and rolled to the work area as needed; it is especially good if you don't have a desk

This window seat cleverly conceals a bank of file cabinet drawers to store important files and records. If you do your paperwork at the dining room table, this is the perfect solution to the problem of where to store the documents that you work with. The unit works equally well in a spare room that serves more than one purpose. Acknowledgment: Design by Kathleen Poer, Spacial Designs, photography by David Wasserman.

and tend to pay bills, etc., at the kitchen or dining room table. If you need more storage than what two drawers will accommodate, you might want to go to a bigger cabinet. Larger cabinets can sometimes be used to divide a room or mark off an area. A lateral cabinet, for example, at the end of a single bed, can be used to hold papers and the television.

Organizing Your Desk

Since home office centers usually feature a desk or workspace of some kind, one of the first places to look at in order to evaluate storage and organization needs is the desk, which all too often invites clutter instead of organization and efficient storage.

To organize your work area, first remove everything from the desk. Next, replace the items using some basic principles that will not only help you organize the desk, but help you *keep* it organized. As you clear the desk, you'll find that at any given time, your desk (and desktop) provides a home to the following items:

- Equipment
- Mail—Incoming and Outgoing
- Personal Items
- Supplies
- Papers and Files

Nearly all of these things can be stored effectively in the desk or work area if you keep the following organizational ideas in mind.

Equipment. Your equipment needs will depend on your use of your office, and can include the telephone, answering machine, typewriter, adding machine, computer, and/or any other equipment that you use on a daily basis. The equipment that always stays on your desk should be placed within easy reach without cluttering the work space of your desk. Ideally, typewriters and computer equipment should be on a stand or return table to either one side of the desk or behind you so that you have a separate work space for typing and computer-related projects.

Mail. All too often the incoming mail buries the outgoing mail, resulting in bills being paid late and important correspondence being lost amidst the piles of paper on the desk. To reduce these potential hazards, have a specific place for incoming mail until you get around to dealing with it. Make sure nothing else gets piled on that spot.

For outgoing mail, you might want to set up a "to go" table or area. Put this table next to the door, and as you get mail ready to go, put it there. Then, when you leave, take it with you. If there is no room for another piece of furniture, or if there's already furniture by the door, such as a filing cabinet, carve out a "to go" spot by putting a basket next to the door either on the floor or on top of the furniture that's already there. A bookcase next to the door can hold a "to go" section if you put a basket on a shelf next to the door, or you can put a red folder marked *out* on the shelf (stand it up in a small plastic letter holder).

Personal Items. Personalized desk accumulation includes (but is not limited to) photographs of children and pets, paperweights, aspirin, jewelry, cash, executive toys and puzzles, keys, awards, teabags, joke statues and plaques, antacid tablets, nail polish, and plants. To keep all of this organized, set aside a small area in one of the drawers for personal items such as aspirin, change, and so forth, and restrict those things to that area only. A photo or two, and a plant can be stored on top of or near the desk for decoration, but if you are tight on space, you won't want to personalize the area any more than that. Be practical—would you benefit more from desktop storage containers for supplies or from extra family photos?

Supplies. Supplies that lurk around the

desk run the gamut from stationery and envelopes to paper clips and pens (many of which often don't work). Round up all of the supplies and get rid of everything that's outdated or doesn't work. You can turn mugs into pencil holders on top of the desk (get rid of broken pens and pencils). Paper clips can be stored on top of the desk in an attractive small dish or in a magnetized paper clip holder. Keep the basics at hand—scissors, stapler, staple remover, tape, and if you use it, hole punch. Everything else should be pared down to just what you use on a daily basis. Typing, computer, and other paper supplies should be kept at hand, but storing a gross of any one item in or around the desk is too space-consuming.

One box of anything if it's small (such as paper clips or rubber bands), and about a fourth of a box of anything large (such as stationery or envelopes) is more than enough to keep in your immediate work area.

A metal or plastic stationery rack will hold paper and envelopes. Generally there are enough compartments in these racks to store other forms that you might use regularly. (For example, if you operate a home-based business, you might have invoice forms and shipping labels for Express Mail that you need to have close at hand.) These holders sit easily on a desk corner or on a credenza behind the desk for easy access whenever you need them. You can also mount file holders over

This modular work station provides work space as well as storage space for files, basic office supplies, reference materials, and computer equipment. Acknowledgment: O'Sullivan Industries.

your desk to hold paper and envelopes. Or you can store paper supplies in the desk file drawer in hanging file folders. There are dividers on the market that you can put into small flat desk drawers, so that you can store the stationery separately layered.

Inside smaller desk drawers, you might want to also put plastic divider trays to help keep the small miscellaneous supplies stored and organized at the same time.

Papers and Files. The piles of papers and files that seem to land on the desk are theoretically those that you are "working on" at that particular time. The reality often is that among those papers and files are often items that need to be filed (another word for stored), tossed (another form of "dead" storage), or put into an envelope and sent out. Magazines, newspapers, and announcements can add to the mess, and before you know it, the top of the desk has vanished. To set up an efficient paper storage system, it's important to establish a paper sorting system. (For more on the Four-Step Paper System, see my book, *How to Get Organized When You Don't Have the Time.*)

The Ultimate in Paper Storage. Finally, I strongly recommend the trash basket as a simple solution to an ugly storage problem. About 80 percent of everything you file never gets looked at again, wasting valuable storage space. Probably 50 percent of the paper you get could be tossed and never missed. After all, much of that paper, such as bills, announcements, and junk mail by the ton will be right back on your doorstep in next week's or next month's mail. Do buy a *large* trash basket. Dinky, prissy little wastebaskets that

A rolling cart is great for organizing large, on-going projects. Acknowledgment: Closet Maid® File Cart by Clairson International.

scream *full* after two or three pieces of junk mail and a couple of wadded up pieces of paper are useless. Keep this large trash basket next to your desk or work area, and if you want to be really clever, put one right outside or inside the door. Then, when you bring the mail into the house, you can dump a lot of it before it ever gets to the home office area where you'll have to figure out where to store it.

Sturdy wire shelving can be adjusted to fit into odd-shaped spaces, providing extra storage space. Acknowledgment: Pelly Industri AB Space Systems.

Chapter 12:
Attic, Basement, and Garage

When it comes to storage problems and solutions, the attic, basement, and garage loom as the final frontier before outside storage units are rented, or a new house with more space is purchased. Of these three, attics probably pose the biggest problem. Access is usually provided by drop-down stairs, or no stairs at all (making a step stool or ladder necessary). Assuming you can successfully navigate this access obstacle, the storage space available in the average attic is limited at best since a pitched roof often means that the side walls provide very little shelf space. In spite of the problems, the average attic owner sooner or later heads for the attic with old military uniforms and unused knickknacks balanced precariously under one arm or on his head.

Basements have stairs as well, and though they are often poorly lit, they tend to be sturdier by far than attic stairs. Nooks and crannies can be plentiful in a basement and can practically call out to be stuffed with cartons of treasures that are, more often than not, pure, unadulterated junk.

The garage, originally designed to protect the automobile from thieves and the elements, is the fastest growing storage solution for many people, particularly western homeowners who don't always have basements or attics. It seems so simple to get the house organized and eliminate unused items by packing the stuff up into cartons and bags, and marching out to the garage where the goods are then "stored." No stairs to fuss with, and it's a simple matter to move the car as the garage fills up. This solution slowly becomes very acceptable, until you really can't remember when the car was ever stored in the garage in the first place.

Whatever type space you have available, it is vital to remember that storing unused items that are never looked at or used serves no other purpose than to take up expensive square footage. Not only that, dirt, bugs, rats, mice, and dampness all conspire to turn treasures into useless junk, regardless of how clean you think you are. Bugs and mice and rats thrive on stacks of things—cartons and papers especially—and dampness (from rain) turns the most priceless clothing and papers into unsalvageable, smelly remnants. Some things are correctly stored in these areas (such as gardening equipment, hardware, tools, paint, and some sports equipment), but most things should never be placed in those areas at all. If you must store other things there, be sure to pack the items carefully in clean, dry boxes, with easy-to-read, large labels on all sides of the box; then store the boxes up off the floor on a dry shelf. Remember, however, that things that are stored for memory's sake need to be stored in the house or given to others who will benefit from the pass-along memory today.

Cabinetry and Shelving

Cabinetry and shelving in the attic, basement,

This shelving can be adjusted to allow for cramped attic space and provides off-the-floor storage for everything from tax records to mementos. Acknowledgment: Professional's Choice™ shelving for the garage.

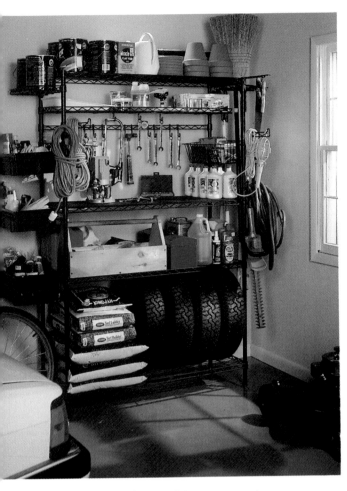

This heavy-duty modular storage system can be assembled in less than ten minutes and creates twenty-four square feet of storage where you need it. Acknowledgment: Professional's Choice™ shelving for the garage

or garage is usually a fairly simple, straightforward affair. Inexpensive industrial metal shelving can hold boxes and bins of things nicely, and can be carried to the area and assembled on the spot. If you don't want to invest in shelving or cabinetry, you can turn an old dresser, cabinet, or bookcase, along with an old table, into a combination storage and work area (the chest can hold tools, for example, and the table will provide a spot for minor repair jobs). Another worktable option is to rest an old hollow-core door across two sawhorses. Hooks and racks on the walls can also be very serviceable, holding everything from garden hoses to bikes. In garages, overhead storage can be found by stretching a door or a large piece of plywood across the beams (where there is space between the beams and the ceiling). In basements, don't forget to consider the space under the stairs where a cabinet, shelving, or an old dresser can be placed to hold either a category of items (such as sports equipment) or some miscellaneous items that need to be stored.

While you're checking out the storage possibilities in these spare areas, you might want to give some serious consideration to exactly how you could more creatively make use of this space (for purposes other than storage).

With some architectural changes, your basement or garage, and even your attic in some cases, could be turned into a rec room, a sewing or hobby room, an office, or a spare guest room. You could still incorporate ample storage space with cabinetry and shelving along with functional furniture, but you'd also have a room to enjoy along with the storage space.

Gardening Equipment

Some people like yard and garden work, and others hate it. Whether you love it or loathe it, yard work of any kind will be easier to face if the supplies and equipment are easy to store and retrieve.

Begin by rounding up all of the gardening supplies, then review the sprays, powders, and poisons, and dispose of outdated materials. Keep these items in a secured cabinet so that children or pets can't get to them. Or you can store these supplies, along with small gardening tools, in a bench that doubles as a storage bin (secure the latch with a padlock). Long-handled tools can be hung on the wall from pressure strips or supported by two or three nails. If you're short on wall space, you can group these tools in a large metal trashcan. Small tools can be stored in bins by category, or, if you only use a few tools, they can be kept in a supply caddy or gardening basket and carried to and from the garden as is. Don't forget overhead garage rafters for storing major equipment that is rarely used (such as out-of-season lawn furniture or the snow shovel, which you can bring down and hand on the wall in the winter). Dowels, or brackets, mounted on the wall, can also hold big items such as wheelbarrows and furniture. Hoses can be stored on a reel with wheels or on a

You can make an attractive and convenient lawn and garden center with this shelving that can be further customized with accessories that can include storage bins, cantilever shelves, and special racks. Acknowledgment: Professional's Choice™ shelving for the garage.

reel mounted next to the water spigot in a garden shed, basement, or garage. Planters and pots are best kept on shelves, with bags of potting soil stored in small covered buckets or trash cans. A worktable near the potting materials can be a definite plus as well.

Hardware

Hardware includes nuts, bolts, screws, picture hangers, wire, nails, and all of the other small assorted handy-Dan stuff that mates indiscriminately in coffee cans, cigar boxes, shoe boxes, and on worktable tops in the garage or basement. Eventually it turns into one big mess that means at least fifteen minutes of digging before the required doodad is located and retrieved.

So before you incorporate any new storage ideas for your hardware, weed out those odd pieces that have been lying around for years, waiting to be used for "something." Once you have eliminated the useless, there are several ways to handle storing the hardware. Metal parts cabinets (available at hardware and some automotive stores) have plastic drawers that are sized to hold screws, nails, nuts and bolts, and the like. Assuming you have the patience to put the nails or screws into the proper drawer when you put them away (as opposed to tossing them into a box or drawer), these can keep your inventory nicely organized. Glass jars of all sorts can also be used effectively to store hardware by size and provide an instant view of what lies within the container. Baby food jars or sample jelly jars are small enough to perfectly store those tiny pieces of hardware that might otherwise get lost in the shuffle. To cut down on the space these jars occupy, install a shelf in the garage or basement, and put some of the jars on the shelf. Attach the lids of the remaining jars to the *underside* of the shelf with a lock washer so that they stay fixed to the shelf. When you need something in one of those jars, unscrew the *jar* instead of the lid, and replace it in the same manner.

If you are using an old dresser or desk for

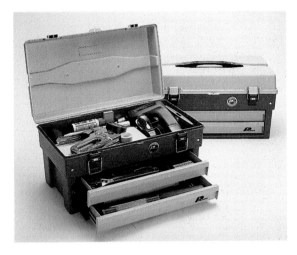

One of the basic tools of organized storage is the tool box. Acknowledgment: Plano Molding Co., Hardware Division, Plano, Illinois.

storage, you can try to keep some order with cutlery dividers in the drawers. Small sample jelly jars also fit into drawers, and you can even put cigar boxes (without the lids) into the drawers to serve as containers for certain categories of items. Boxes and bins can be useful for hardware that is stored on shelves. Cigar boxes, small gift boxes, coffee cans, tea tins, plastic shoe boxes, and plastic bins can all be stacked to hold hardware on a shelf. Be sure to mark the outside of the box or bin on all sides (i.e., *screws, wire, large nails*), so you don't have to check every box to get to the one you need for any given project.

Tools

Essential tools can be stored in a number of ways. A conventional tool box will do the trick and can be stored on a shelf or in a cabinet; a metal parts cabinet can hold smaller tools as well. If you've got only a few items, store

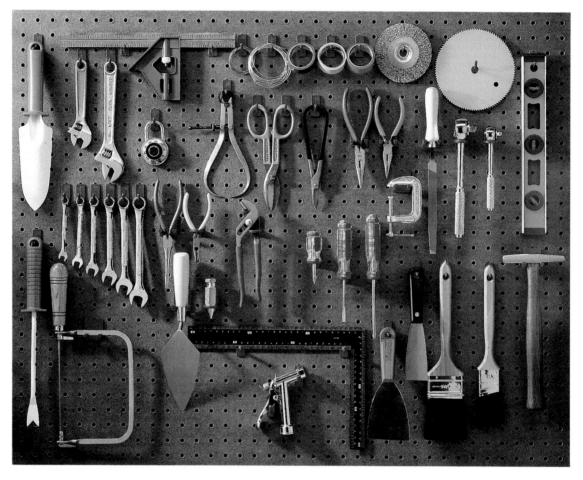

You can turn wall space into a tool center with this pegboard and hook system. Acknowledgment: Rubbermaid's Work Space™ System.

them in a sturdy box or in a plastic kitty litter pan, which can be placed on a shelf, table, or in a cabinet. If you're a real Mr. or Ms. Fixit, you'll want to store the tools next to a worktable in the garage or basement by putting a table next to some storage shelving or cabinetry. Many tools can be hung on the wall from a pegboard and hook system or with nails. To help insure that the tools are kept where they belong, you can make an outline of each tool directly onto the wall so it's easy for anyone to replace the tools properly. Organizing the tools can be a breeze—you can separate the tools easily enough by putting all of the screwdrivers into a coffee can, for instance. (A locked cabinet is best for storing tools if there are small children about, however.) Only put useful tools into your tool/work center in the garage or basement, and remember to store them safely and sensibly, and your tool storage problem should solve itself.

Paint and Paintbrushes

Everyone feels that they have to keep paint and paintbrushes because, after all, that's the color we used for the den or the masterpiece that we made for Aunt Em. Paint cans and brushes accumulate in the garage or basement or in some cabinet, with the contents slowly solidifying as we blissfully ignore the problem as long as possible.

The best way to keep on top of the paint problem is to follow some simple storage principles. First, know that ignoring the stuff is just asking for trouble. Next, get rid of the paint you never use, deal with paint you do use properly every time you use it, and never buy any more than you need in the first place. Unless you're preparing to undertake a major painting project, don't keep more than a quart of paint on hand. You don't need more than that turning into concrete at any given time. Any leftover paint should be clearly marked and stored on a shelf or in a cabinet. If there are children about, a secured cabinet is a good idea. Brushes can be hung on a hook or nail or stored, brush up, in coffee cans. Stored in this manner, they dry a little better after you've cleaned them, increasing your chances of being able to reuse them.

Finally, and perhaps most importantly, when you get rid of paint, be sure to follow environmental requirements in your area for toxic disposal. (See page 100 for details on safe disposal of toxic household wastes.) And, before you toss any paint, make a note of the color and the room it was used in so that you can match it later if necessary.

Sports Equipment

Sports equipment tends to get jammed into closets, corners, and, most of the time, basements and garages. When you need something, you've got sports gear scattered everywhere and you can't find the one thing you need. Before you start sorting, be a sport and streamline your sports storage equipment by first getting rid of anything you no longer use. If your kid's Babe Ruth days are long gone, give that baseball equipment to a kid just entering that phase. If you broke your leg the last time you skied and swore you'd never ski again, get rid of the skis and take up something less adventurous.

The equipment that you use with some regularity should be stored in one area in the basement or garage. (An alternative to this is to turn a closet in the house — such as the hall closet — into a sports storage center, or to store the children's sports gear in their room.) Everything from skis to bicycles can be mounted on the wall, so if you've got the wall space, this is a good way to go. The rafters in a garage can hold out-of-season skis as well. A large, clean trash can will accommodate balls and bats. Tennis rackets can be hung on hooks on a pegboard system on the wall, and special protective gear, like kneepads and catcher's masks, can be stored in a drawer, a large bin, a chest, or a footlocker. A freestanding wardrobe can hold sports gear in one area as well. If your exercise gear is in the basement or garage, devote one corner for that equipment and don't worry about putting it away. If you have to put it away and drag it out every time you use it, you'll find excuses not to exercise. However you handle storing your sports equipment, once you've established a "sports center" it's a simple matter to find what you need and to put the equipment away when you're finished with it.

In the end, the attic, garage, and basement represent the final frontier for storage, so once you've tackled the storage problem in those areas, you'll want to think twice about what you store there in the future. Using those areas as a dumping ground for things that you aren't ready to part with only means you are postponing your eventual day of reckoning. Remember that the next time you clean out a closet in the house and find yourself heading to the attic, basement, or garage, with a box or bag of things to be "stored."

Tips from the Pros
Jody Sibert, Up from Under

With more than six years' experience as a Professional Organizer under her belt, Jody Sibert, owner of the organizational firm, Up from Under  in Venice, California, has added another dimension to her repertoire of organizational and storage consultation services: ecology. She combines her concerns for the environment and her client's health with her abilities as an organizer to provide advice not only on how to organize and store things, but also on how to eliminate toxic substances that may be stored in the house, garage, attic, or basement. Although even common household cleaning products can have some level of toxicity, she also points out that some extremely hazardous materials are also likely to be stored in the garage, attic, or basement. Her tips for ecologically sound organization and storage include:

● **Paint.** Exposure to some paint, paint thinners, and paint removers that contain solvents can cause everything from central nervous systems disorders to birth defects and cancer. If your paint is oil based or if it contains methylene chloride (a highly toxic substance), you should contact your community's hazardous waste collection program. If, however, you have some unusable leftover latex paints, remove the lids, place the cans in a well-ventilated area, and when the contents are solidified, you can replace the lid on the can and throw it in the trash. *Do not pour the paint down the drain.* If you have usable leftover paint that does not match the paint in your home, you can donate it to schools and theatre groups.

● **Automotive Products.** Automotive products stored in your garage may also be harmful. Motor oil and transmission brake fluids contain poisonous chemical compounds. Car batteries are highly acidic and can cause serious burns, and motor oil and batteries can also contain lead. Leftover motor oil should be taken to a service station, or you can call the highway department for the name of your nearest oil recycling center. Take dead batteries to your local shop to see about a trade in. And never store gasoline at home. Take it to your hazardous waste collection center. (If your community doesn't have a hazardous waste collection center, call the city disposal service to get guidelines from them for disposal of those items.)

● **Gardening Supplies.** Many pesticides are poisonous and highly dangerous for people, pets, and wildlife. The value of pesticides and chemical fertilizers over the long term to the environment is debatable, so Sibert urges you to research alternative organic methods for your gardening needs. All pesticides and fertilizers that are ready for disposal should be disposed through your hazardous waste collection agency. *Never, ever, pour them down the drain or put them in the trash.*

Sibert offers these final tips:

Don't buy more than you need. That way, you'll avoid having to dispose of the surplus. Give leftovers away to groups or neighbors who have use for them. And never repackage anything in other containers without making up new warning labels for the new container. If you are in doubt about disposal methods, consult your Yellow Pages under *recycling center* or *waste disposal.* You can also do some research into your local environmental agencies, and contact them for further information. Or you can call the U.S. Consumer Product Safety Center (1-800-638-CPSC), and they will provide you with more information on household chemical hazards.

A well-planned investment, this bathroom cabinetry provides maximum storage space as well as elegance for the bath. Acknowledgment: Wood-Mode Cabinetry.

Chapter 13:
The Plan

Now that you've completed the walking tour of your house and given some thought to your storage needs, it's time to couple those creative ideas with some carefully planned action. Working on one room at a time, you can follow this Eight-Step Plan to give you the storage you need, whether it is in your bedroom, kitchen, home office, or entire home. Be prepared to invest a little time, some money, and a lot of patience into this project, because whatever the scope of your storage requirements, you're almost certain to find yourself at some point dealing with time, money, and the need for patience to get you through the process. But the benefits will more than make up for any sacrifices. You'll have more organized storage for your possessions, which will put things at your fingertips when you need them and keep other things stored efficiently when you don't. Your new storage can be beautifully incorporated into your decor or design scheme, and with some thoughtful planning, can take you well into the future to handle not only your storage needs of today but also those needs that will develop several years from now.

Eight Steps to Successful Storage

Step 1: Clear Out the Clutter

Begin by taking inventory of everything that you now have stored as well as the things you would like to store. Room by room, go through everything in dressers, cabinets, closets, and corners. To do this effectively, you'll need to set up the proper attitude and atmosphere. Use the following guidelines to get you through this all-important first step:

Don't allow distractions. No visitors, TV, or stopping to read an article in a magazine you pick up. No phone calls, either—don't take any and don't make any. Unplug the phone so you won't be tempted to answer it. You need to concentrate fully on the task at hand. Finally, *Stay out of the kitchen!* Stop to eat only if it is breakfast, lunch, or dinnertime. Constant snacking equals procrastination and pounds.

Do one thing at a time. If you are cleaning out a closet, just work on that closet; don't walk into another room and start doing something else until you are finished with that closet. To help you in this endeavor, set up cartons labeled *charity, toss, mending,* and *elsewhere.* As you come across things that should go into another room, put them in the *elsewhere* box and distribute those things at the end of the day. Otherwise, you'll end up running all over the house, interrupting yourself over and over as you transfer items to other rooms.

Be decisive. Decide to decide what you are going to do with each item you find. Quit making excuses for keeping things that you really don't need. *Use it or lose it.* If you're not using it, get rid of it. Period.

You also need to learn to let go. As lives change, needs change, but somehow our possessions accumulate with no regard to our changed perspective. Things that are merely taking up valuable space and giving you nothing in return should be tossed or given away.

Resolve to give things away, right away. Don't wait until you die to give that china away if you never use it now when you are alive. Every garment hanging in your closet that you never wear could be worn by a less fortunate person every day. Remember that friends, relatives, and charities all appreciate a giving person far more than they do a pack rat.

Dump the junk. At the end of the organizing session, immediately transfer *charity* items to your favorite charity, and throw items in the *toss* box away before other family members (or you) have the chance to start digging through the box to rescue some useless treasure. The *mending* goes straight to the tailor or seamstress, or it goes to *charity*. If you have a pile of mending that's been around for ages because you were going to "get to it someday," someday has arrived. Let someone else do it once and for all, or get rid of it altogether.

Group like things together. The belongings that are left after this weeding-out process stay in the room, grouped by category (all the sweaters together, all the games in one area, all the sports gear together, etc.). You'll save time and aggravation if you have to go to only one storage "center" to get what you need for any activity.

Seek professional help if necessary. If you've got several years' worth of clutter that a professional can help you get through in a few days, it can be well worth the expense. And it can give you a terrific start on streamlining your storage requirements, since the organizer will help you decide what to get rid of so you won't be tempted to build more storage than you really need.

Step 2: A Place for Everything

A place for everything and everything in its place is the perfect axiom for effective storage. Once you've weeded out excess clutter, assess your activities as they relate to your storage needs.

For example, if you dabble in art and you are researching the family tree, you will need storage space at least for art supplies and for resource files for your family tree project. You might want to map this information out on paper first, prioritizing the most important projects so that you can match up storage needs by priority as well. Then begin assigning areas for the items related to that activity to be stored. For example, your clothing (but only the clothing you actually wear regularly) obviously goes in or near your closet. Your art projects, on the other hand, need to be assigned an "art center" storage and work space; that could be an area in a spare room, one-third of the area in your studio apartment, or a working corner in the dining room. Or maybe you want to make the linen closet your art center (you can put the linens in the bathroom or in the bedrooms where they will eventually wind up anyway). The important thing is to assign a place for everything, and then put everything in its place.

To decide where things go, try to keep items as close to their point of use as possible. Dishes should be in cabinets near the sink or dishwasher. Videotapes should be near the VCR. Paper and pens belong near the telephone or in the desk. Recipes should be in the kitchen. Some things may need more storage space than others. If you have a lot of sports gear, for example, you may need to consider customizing your spare closet to hold all of the equipment. If you are an avid gardener, a gardening storage and work center in the garage can make a tremendous difference in your gardening on a daily basis.

Storing duplicate items can also be helpful. Keeping scissors in the bathroom and on the desk can eliminate searching for and moving the scissors around every time you need to clip something. Don't carry this duplicate concept too far, however. In the kitchen, you probably don't need duplicates of whisks, pastry blenders, or other utensils and miscellaneous doodads.

As you assign storage sites to your things according to the purpose of those belongings in your life, you will no doubt have some things that you simply can't get rid of; they require storage even though they are not used. Off-season clothing, business records that are required by law to be kept for a certain number of years, outdoor furniture that is out of season, and some out-of-season sports gear are examples of things that need to be stored, even though they are temporarily "dead." These items should be stored in areas that are not necessarily immediately accessible. For instance, the outdoor furniture can be stored on platforms suspended across the garage raf-

A mug rack mounts easily to the hall closet door to hold hats, scarves, bags, and umbrellas. Acknowledgment: Lillian Vernon Catalogue.

ters. Out-of-season sports gear can be stored in a locker in the basement. Old love letters or important tax records can be boxed and placed on an upper shelf in a spare closet, or if necessary, stored in the attic.

Step 3: Using Containers Creatively

As you put your things in assigned areas, grouped by category, look around the house for baskets, bins, and containers that you can use to help hold things in those areas. Baskets can be attractive and functional at the same time. Square or oblong baskets are the best bet since they hold more in less space than do round baskets. Decorative tins, plastic bins, dishpans, and kitty litter pans along with plastic shoe and sweater boxes can all do a good job of holding groups of items. You can use these containers to store a plethora of things in any given area. Containers and baskets provide homes for cosmetics, yarn and crochet supplies, dirty and clean laundry, postcards and greeting cards, magazines and newspapers, jewelry, toys, stuffed animals, pens and pencils, coupons, hair ornaments and pins, vacuum cleaner parts, and much, much more. Your imagination will help you put what you already have to good storage use; what containers you still need can be purchased at any number of shops and from catalogs that sell organizing products. (Subsequent steps in your planning process, along with the Resource Guide at the back of the book will help you decide on what purchases to make to meet your specific needs.)

Step 4: Taking Measurements

Now that you've weeded out the excess, allocated specific places for groups of items, and made effective use of organizational storage containers, review your storage areas to see where you need to add more space. Perhaps installing a double-rod system in your closet for your separates would give you enough hanging room for all of your clothes (so they won't get crushed). Or, perhaps you need some cabinetry in the spare room to hold your craft supplies. Maybe you'd like some shelving or cabinets in the garage to hold your gardening equipment or tools. You could be short on adequate space in the bathroom, and feel that shelves would do the trick for storing linen and excess grooming aids. Before you install shelving or cabinetry, take accurate measurements so you can accurately assess your needs and project the budget required. To measure available wall space or interior closet or cabinet space so that you can add shelving or install organizational systems and/or cabinetry, keep these guidelines in mind:

Record interior dimensions. Measure the height, width, and depths for all of your cabinet and closet interiors. Note all allowances and clearances required in the measurements. Be especially careful when measuring for hanging racks or shelves on the inside of cabinets. Also measure inside drawers so that you can find dividers or drawer trays to fit them for organized drawer storage. And measure your largest possessions, so that you can more accurately determine the total amount of space required to store those things comfortably. Make sure you allow extra space for future purchases and expansion.

Climb the walls. Measure wall space and cabinet door space (both sides) for storage possibilities with pegboard or grid and hook systems. Make sure that anything you install on doors will not hit the shelves when the door is shut. Also, check the construction of walls before you attempt to install attached shelving. Different surfaces require different hardware and treatment. Talk to your hardware representative for guidance.

Note architectural fixtures. Remember

to indicate in your measurements where the windows begin and end, pipe placement, outlet placement (so you don't block the outlet), heating and air conditioning vents, and so forth. And don't forget room to *move*. Always allow clearance space for traffic and easy access to all areas of the room. Take into account the amount of space required to open drawers, doors, and baskets (on rolling basket systems).

If you plan to use basket systems or bins on casters, measure the available floor space along with the clearance space at the top of the basket; also allow for the space required when the basket is extended out from the unit.

Do it yourself. Measure all odd-sized spaces or belongings before you go shopping for systems. You might stumble across something that will fit in that space or that will accommodate an especially odd-shaped item. Finally, obtain the measurements of the systems that you might install yourself (such as a basket system) and match those measurements to the measurements that you have of your available space.

Step 5: Establishing a Budget

Now that you've done all you can do with what you've got, and measured areas that can be improved with additional storage systems, it's time to take a look at what your budget can handle. You can spend a few dollars or thousands of dollars—today the storage possibilities are so extensive that the sky is the limit for the consumer. Based on cost, you may want to begin by just adding a few shelves here and there (installing them yourself with brackets and standards). Or you may want to purchase a small selection of organizational systems, such as racks, bins, and portable shelf extenders. These steps will no doubt help you, but more than likely, it won't be enough to take you very far into the future. A newly installed closet system and/or the addition of a wall unit or some extra cabinetry can cost a significant amount of money, but the result can increase your storage space significantly, adding to the resale value of your home. (Naturally, if you are in a rented apartment, you will want to buy only portable

This portable storage and work utility cart can add much needed functional space to the kitchen. Acknowledgment: Photograph courtesy of Hold Everything Catalogue.

things that you can take with you when you move; i.e., you may do better with portable basket systems and a few self-installed shelving units rather than all fixed systems in the closet.)

There are closet designers and installers aplenty now, so it pays to shop around. Usually, these shops will send someone out to assess your organizational needs in terms of available space only (they won't get into your storage needs as it applies to your lifestyle; they simply look at the closet or other space that needs to be maximized, and tell you what they can do with it). Based on your budget, you can have them install all or part of the systems that you will need to enhance your storage space.

At the high end of the custom market are space-planning experts who can turn walk-in closets, wall closets, or entire rooms or storage facilities into virtual works of functional art tailored specifically to your needs. Generally, these people charge a fee for an initial consultation, and their fees thereafter are hourly to draw up the designs. After that, you can usually go with their custom cabinetmaker or your own, or you can sometimes simply pay for the plans and try to get a less expensive closet shop to do the installation with their materials. This last option can be tricky, though, since most moderately priced closet installers work with precut pieces of material, and while they do make adjustments, most of them are within standard linear foot guidelines. The top space planners, on the other hand, match their creativity to each project, and often this creativity is best realized by a professional custom cabinet-

maker.

If you decide to work with a professional, be clear about your expectations as well as your budget in the beginning. Bear in mind that although a professional may cost more than doing it yourself, in the end you may have the bonus of even more storage space, since a professional can very often maximize your current storage space much better than you can. Finding an extra four square feet in a closet can make the difference between clothes that are always squashed and just a bit wrinkled, and clothes that hang neatly and never need last-minute pressing.

Step 6: By Design

Designing additional storage space is the final step before you purchase additional storage equipment or install space-saving systems. With your measurements and your budget in mind, consider the following options as you and/or your closet designer decide on the system that will be best for you:

Adapting Closets and Spare Spaces. Some closets can be used in any number of ways. A large closet can be turned into an office or study area, or a small playroom. Spare spaces can be used for storage or hobby areas; check halls, foyers, and spaces under hall stairs for possible extra space. Check the walls and rafters in the garage and the area under the stairs in the basement for adaptable space. Finally, remember that a linen closet need not be used for linens, and a coat closet isn't just for coats. A little creativity goes a long way with spare space and closet adaptation.

Purpose. Decide what the primary pur-

Tips from the Pros
John Sarandon, The Closet Store

John Sarandon was among the first in the country to capitalize on the need for space-saving storage and closet systems. In 1981, he opened The Closet Store in Los Angeles to serve that need. Today, he has two locations and a warehouse in the Los Angeles area. The Closet Store specializes in space planning for closet interiors and space-saving products for closets and the kitchen area. Over the years, The Closet Store has installed thousands of systems into walk-in and wardrobe closets, linen closets, utility closets, kids' closets, and garage work areas. Sarandon offers these guidelines to help you shop around for the best installation of storage systems:

• **Find out how long the company has been in business.** There are lots of closet installers today, but some are here today and gone tomorrow. Make sure the company you deal with has a solid reputation.

• **Ask for references of completed projects.** Ask those references if they were happy with the way the job was installed, and if the results met their expectations.

• **Ask about product warranty.** For example, The Closet Store's product line includes laminated systems and furniture from Techline, who warranties their product unconditionally for three years, and conditionally for ten years. The Closet Store guarantees their installation for one year.

Products and prices for closet and storage systems vary, depending on where you live and who you deal with. Here's what you can expect to find:

• **Vinyl Coated Wire Shelving and Basket Systems.** These ventilated systems allow air to flow through them and provide clear visibility for spotting things on upper shelves. No painting maintenance is required, and they are generally very easy to move (if you move). You can expect to pay from five dollars to nine dollars per linear foot for this system.

• **Laminated Systems.** These systems are composed of an easy-to-wash laminated material which is hot pressed over pressed wood. Generally available in a sleek modern white, they are usually fully adjustable, with shelves and rods that are easy to move to different positions as your needs change. You can expect to pay from forty dollars to sixty dollars per linear foot for this system.

• **Custom Wood.** Custom-cut wood products can mean anything from do-it-yourself plywood to exotic woods and finishes. The results can be breathtaking, and for homes with entire rooms given over to wardrobe storage, this is often the preferred method of approaching the storage problem and design. You'll need a qualified space planner or architect to draw up the plans for your design and a cabinetmaker to install the system. The cost, not only for the wood and finishes but also for the professional services, can be quite high. They sky's the limit here.

Sarandon offers one last bit of advice: don't expect miracles. You can't get the same results in terms of storage capacity with a five-foot closet as you can with a ten-foot or a walk-in closet. And if you aren't organized or are a compulsive pack rat, a new system is only part of the answer to your problem. The rest of the solution is entirely up to you.

109

pose of the room is, and build your storage to suit that purpose. If a spare room is going to be a sewing room, add storage for that only. If the room serves more than one purpose, be sure to allocate specific areas within the room for each activity and the storage requirements that go along with it.

Traffic. Keep traffic patterns in mind. You don't want to block walkways or make it inconvenient to get to items that are used on a daily basis. Storage facilities should not block traffic patterns; they should be adjacent to them.

Use Wall Space Effectively. Where storage space is tight, consider floor-to-ceiling wall units which can be used to hold any number of things, from games, hobby supplies, and bins of toys, to books, record albums, cassettes, and entertainment equipment. Hooks, pegs, and racks can also be wall-mounted to hold clothes, towels, sports gear, pots and pans, and more.

Open vs. Closed Storage. Decide whether you want open or closed cabinetry or shelving, or a mix of both. Items that are meant for display (such as books, antiques, and knickknacks) need to be on open shelving or displayed on furniture tops (like the piano or perhaps the fireplace mantle). Things that are used regularly need to be kept in open storage or behind cabinet doors that are easy to access. Things that are virtually never used, like past tax records, can be stashed in out-of-the-way closed storage—the back or top shelves of a closet, for instance—thus using space that might otherwise be overlooked.

Built-in vs. Freestanding Storage. Decide whether you want built-in or freestanding cabinetry and shelving for storage. Freestanding is substantially less expensive than built-in, but custom-built cabinetry can also save you significantly more space than can some of the freestanding storage units on the market. Of course, if you rent rather than own, chances are you will want to opt for freestanding rather than custom built-ins so that you can take your storage units with you if and when you move. In any case, some freestanding units such as the basket systems are so useful that it more than justifies the purchase, since you can use it in one area for a time and then elsewhere when it outgrows its original purpose.

Functional Furniture. If you are planning to buy furniture in the near future, make sure it's functional. Bedside tables that have shelves or drawers as well as hold the lamp and clock radio are just as attractive as a bedside table with no storage. End tables, coffee tables, chests, and entertainment centers can all do double duty as furniture and storage; adapt buffets, armoires, and trunks for innovative storage solutions. Armoires can be entertainment centers and buffets can hold home office supplies; trunks can hold memorabilia and also serve daily as a coffee table or end table when topped with a piece of glass.

Step 7: Installation and Organization

Once you and/or your space planner or closet designer have decided on additional storage systems, installation and organization completes the design process. Clear everything out of the area marked for new installations, and if you are doing it yourself, make sure you plan to complete each area all at once. It can

This easy-to-install wire closet system features specific areas of storage for foldables, shoes, ties, separates, dresses and coats, and other miscellaneous things that are often stored temporarily in a closet. Acknowledgment: Closet King® Specialty Retail Stores, New York City.

be very disruptive, for example, to have the entire closet emptied, with everything on the bed while the closet is being redone. Keeping the time required for the installation down to a minimum lessens the overall aggravation that seems to accompany the nuts-and-bolts reality of any type of renovation process. If someone else is doing the installation, make sure that dates and deadlines are clearly understood and agreed upon.

Once the new systems are installed, it's up to you to put everything back, organizing your belongings neatly as they are returned to their storage area. Be sure that you store like items together and store things near their point of first use. Creating storage "centers" as you put things away will make organizational maintenance in the future much simpler for everyone. Shoving things onto shelves and behind closet and cabinet drawers in a disorganized fashion is counterproductive and ultimately wastes space. As with the beginning of this process, if you have a problem with this, you may want to hire a professional organizer to put everything back together for you. A good organizer will be able to put everything away neatly and in the proper area, giving you a fresh start with organized, efficient storage of your possessions. Once your possessions have been put away properly, it should be far easier for you to keep the system organized.

Step 8: Keeping Your Closets and Storage Organized

Now that you've weeded out and organized all of your belongings, and created effective storage for them, it's up to you to keep it that way—*organized and effectively stored.*

To make sure your storage requirements don't exceed the space you have available for that purpose, try living (and storing) by these fundamental principles:

- Implement simple storage systems that will grow with your needs.
- Don't buy anything you don't need, and don't buy anything unless you have a specific place to put it when you get home.
- Use the In & Out Inventory Rule. When something new comes in, something old goes out.
- Don't buy things just because they are on sale. You have to find storage space for them, regardless of the price.
- Set limits on how many new toys the kids can get on nonoccasion days. Make them live by the In & Out Inventory Rule as well.
- Use it or lose it.
- Continually (or at least twice a year) weed out clothing that is out of date or doesn't fit you.
- Don't hang onto broken appliances that take up storage space but can't be used.
- Use the Four-Step Paper System to keep your daily papers sorted and stored efficiently. (See page 91).
- Think before you file that piece of paper. Eighty percent of everything you file you never look at again.
- Don't store things for other people. You need that storage space for yourself.
- Make each family member responsible for his or her own personal storage areas.
- Don't use the garage or basement as a storage dumping ground. You are only postponing the day of reckoning, since you'll have to deal with all of the stuff you've stored there sooner or later.

Finally, if you find yourself running out of room, forget about moving. Just stop and spend some time weeding out and organizing your belongings. A good de-junking every six

This wall unit conceals stereo equipment and accessories in functional pull-outs, turning it into an easy-to-use entertainment center. Acknowledgment: Wood-Mode Cabinetry.

months or so can keep you on top of the storage problem altogether.

Much success!

If you've got a perplexing storage problem or a creative storage solution, I'd like to hear from you. You may write me at:

Stephanie Culp
The Organization
P.O. Box 996
Montrose, CA 91021

About the Author

Organization and time management consultant Stephanie Culp is the author of several books, including *How to Get Organized When You Don't Have the Time,* and *How to Conquer Clutter.* She is the owner of the organization and management consulting firm, THE ORGANIZATION in Los Angeles. Her firm designs and implements systems and establishes procedures to help businesses and people get, and stay, organized.

As a national speaker and seminar leader, she has helped thousands of people help themselves get organized. She is also the publisher of *Organizing News,* a newsletter that features organizing and management tips and techniques for personal and professional lifestyles. Her articles have also appeared in several national publications, and she is a contributor to the *Los Angeles Times.*

Culp served as a delegate to the White House Conference on Small Business and she is a founding member and past President of the National Association of Professional Organizers, where she was the recipient of an award for her outstanding contribution to the field of organizing.

Other Books by Stephanie Culp

How to Get Organized When You Don't Have the Time, 216 pages, $10.95, paperback

How to Conquer Clutter, 176 pages, $10.95, paperback

To order, send the price of the book, plus $3.00 postage and handling for one book, 50¢ for each additional book, to:

Writer's Digest Books
1507 Dana Avenue
Cincinnati, OH 45207

Credit card orders call TOLL-FREE
1-800-289-0963
(Ohio residents add 5½% sales tax.)

Resource Guide

Acme Display Fixture Co.
1057 Olive Street
Los Angeles, CA 90015
Hangers and closet fixtures.

Alpak Industries
185 Route 17
Mahwah, NJ 07430
Corrugated storage products.

Armstrong World Industries, Inc.
P. O. Box 3001
Lancaster, PA 17601
Ready-to-assemble furniture.

Atlantic Representations, Inc.
141 North Clark Drive, #2
Los Angeles, CA 90048
Wire storage products.

Black & Decker
6 Armstrong Road
Sheffon, CT 06484
Appliances for kitchen and home.

British Design Corp.
8200 Capwell Drive
Oakland, CA 94621
Two-shelf etagere.

Clairson International
720 South West 17th Street
Ocala, FL 32674
Manufacturer of organizing systems.

Closet King®
880 Lexington Avenue
New York, NY 10022
Closet systems and planning service.

Corr-Pak International
19 Kimberly Lane
East Brunswick, NJ 08816
Closet storage accessories.

Cosmepak
Hanover Avenue & Horsehill Road
P. O. Box 1907
Morristown, NJ 07960-1907
Bath and cosmetic organizers.

Equipto
225 South Highland Avenue
Aurora, IL 60507
Steel workshop shelving.

Fellowes Manufacturing Co.
1789 Norwood Avenue
Itasca, IL 60143
Corrugated organizers.

Grayline Housewares
1616 Berkley Street
Elgin, IL 60123
Wire organizational products.

Gusdorf Corporation
11440 Lackland Road
St. Louis, MO 63146
Wire organizational products.

Hold Everything
Williams Sonoma
Catalogue Mail Order Department
P. O. Box 7807
San Francisco, CA 94120-7807
Organizing and storage products (catalog).

Intermetro Industries Corp.
Professional's Choice
North Washington Street
Wilkes-Barre, PA 18705
Modular storage systems.

Kaleidoscope Design, Inc.
1755 North Oak Road
P. O. Box 699
Plymouth, IN 46563-0699
Tubular furniture for kids.

Kohler Co.
Kohler, WI 53044
Plumbing and specialty bath products.

Linda London
London Closets
200 East 62nd Street
New York, NY 10021
Custom closet interiors.

Merillat Industries, Inc.
5353 West U.S. 223 Highway
Adrian, MI 49221
Nation's largest manufacturer of cabinetry.

Metropolitan Vacuum Cleaner Co., Inc.
One Ramapo Avenue
P. O. Box 149
Suffern, NY 10901
Vacuum cleaner attachment holder.

Modulus
2023 West Carroll Avenue
Chicago, IL 60612
Organization and space-saving products.

Murphy Door Bed Co., Inc.
5300 New Horizons Blvd.
Amityville, NY 11701
Folding wall beds.

National Kitchen and Bath Association
124 Main Street
Hackettstown, NJ 07840
Association of kitchen and bath planners.

Maxine Ordesky
Organized Designs
240 South Linden Drive
Beverly Hills, CA 90212
Custom space planning and design.

O'Sullivan Industries, Inc.
1900 Gulf Street
Lamar, MO 64759
Storage furniture and cabinetry.

Pelly Industri AB
P. O. Box 70
S-330 33 Hillerstorp
SWEDEN
Wire storage systems.

Plano Molding Co.
431 East South Street
Plano, IL 60545
Tackle, tool, and cosmetic organizers.

Pottery Barn
Mail Order Department
P. O. Box 7044
San Francisco, CA 94120-7044
Home furnishings and decorative items (catalog).

Kathleen Poer
Spacial Design
21 Pamaron Way, Suite A
Novato, CA 94949
Space organization and design.

Romanoff Design
156 Fifth Avenue, Suite 1100
New York, NY 10010
Storage boxes and wire racks.

Rosti (USA) Inc.
18 Sidney Circle
Kenilworth, NJ 07033
Complete line of housewares.

Lee Rowan
Consumer Affairs
6333 Etzel Avenue
St. Louis, MO 63133
Home and closet organizing products.

Rubbermaid, Incorcoprated
1147 Akron Road
Wooster, OH 44691
Storage products for the home and workshop.

Rutt Custom Kitchens
1564 Main Street
P. O. Box 129
Goodville, PA 17528
Ellipse Deluxe kitchen cabinetry.

John Sarandon Enterprises
The Closet Store
2801 South Robertson Blvd.
Los Angeles, CA 90034
Storage space planning and installation.

S & B Resources, Inc.
28956 Orchard Lake Road
Farmington Hills, MI 48018
Hang-up closet fixture.

Scanimport America, Inc.
1309 Travis Avenue
Staten Island, NY 10314
Norscan® wire storage systems.

Selfix, Inc.
4501 West 47th Street
Chicago, IL 60632
Storage organizing systems.

Jody Sibert
Up from Under
577 Grand Blvd.
Venice, CA 90291
Professional organizer.

Space Systems, Inc.
48435 Bayshore Drive
Belleville, MI 48111
Wire closet and storage systems.

Spectrum Diversified Designs
P. O. Box 46626
Cleveland, OH 44146
Storage and organization products.

Taylor & Ng
1212 B 19th Street
Oakland, CA 94607
Kitchen storage racks.

Techline
by Marshall Erdman & Associates
5117 University Avenue
Madison, WI 53705
Furniture, cabinetry, and closet systems.

Thomasville Industries, Inc.
P. O. Box 319
Thomasville, GA 31799
Butcher-block furniture.

Tomorrow Companies
(The Tomorrow Group, Inc.)
991 Broadway
Albany, NY 12204
The Wall Grabber wall unit.

Lillian Vernon Catalog
510 South Fulton Avenue
Mount Vernon, NY 10550
Organizational and storage products (catalog).

Wallbeds Plus
113 South Robertson Blvd.
Los Angeles, CA 90048
Wall beds and modules.

Wood Mode Cabinetry
#1 Second Street
Kreamer, PA 17833
Custom cabinetry.

Zenith Products, Corp.
200 Commerce Drive
Aston, PA 19014
Storage space savers.

Index